FERRY TALES

of Argyll and the Isles

D1390469

To Gay
who inspired me to live fully
and who is teaching me to see

FERRY TALES

of Argyll and the Isles

Walter Weyndling

Birlinn

This revised and expanded edition published in 2003
by Birlinn Limited
West Newington House
10 Newington Road
Edinburgh EH9 1QS

Reprinted 2007

First published in 1996 by Alan Sutton Publishing Ltd, Stroud

ISBN 13 978 1 84158 270 2
ISBN 10 1 84158 270 0

British Library Cataloguing in Publication Data
A catalogue record for this book is available from the British Library

Typesetting and origination by Brinnoven, Livingston
Printed and bound by Antony Rowe Ltd, Chippenham, Wiltshire

CONTENTS

FOREWORD

Cha toir cas mi dh'Innis Ghall
(I cannot go to the Hebrides on foot)

These words from a song attributed to a daughter of MacNeill of Barra, married to a nobleman on the Scottish mainland, eloquently illustrate the fact that sea transport and the human history of Scotland's western seaboard are inextricably linked. Evidence drawn from archaeological, documentary and oral sources as well as place-name studies shows how the need for good communication routes has dominated the world-view and activities of the inhabitants of its island and mainland communities from the earliest times to the present day.

This is a story of vessels, the craft that connected one place with another, and of people: those who designed and built them, captained and crewed them, serviced and maintained them, and travelled and depended upon them. And here the teller combines material drawn from printed and archival sources with the fruits of almost fifty years of professional involvement and personal fascination with the subject.

Walter Weyndling was born in Cracow, Poland, where his father was an architect, in 1921. There he attended the same school as Josef Conrad and from an early age his imagination too was captured by the sea. Poor eyesight prevented him from pursuing a naval career but from the age of fourteen he determined that he would come to Glasgow, that pre-eminent centre of marine engineering, to study shipbuilding. He achieved his goal and in 1939 joined a Glasgow University class to study with Professor Percy Hillhouse, designer of the 'Empress' boats. Concurrently he undertook an apprenticeship as a shipwright in the Connell yard at Scotstoun. He graduated with first class honours in 1943.

Between 1943 and 1947 he was first in the Royal Air Force, then with the Naval Construction Department of the Admiralty at Bath designing aircraft carriers and at a Middlesbrough shipyard as an Assistant Naval Architect. From 1948 to 1953, however, he worked as a Marine Surveyor with the Board of Trade on the East Coast of Scotland, based at Leith, and looking after the area from Eyemouth to St Monans for five years. Following a short spell in London he returned to Scotland, taking up a post on the West Coast, based on the Clyde, and for twenty years he travelled the sea routes of its lower reaches, throughout Argyll and beyond.

The Board of Trade had oversight of a range of vessels from passenger liners to pleasure craft, as well as fishing boats, barges, puffers and other small cargo boats, and ferries. Only the big cargo ships were excluded, being the remit of Lloyds of London. Walter Weyndling was thus responsible for 'almost everything that floated'. His visits to the ports and havens of the west coast were always keenly anticipated locally, for his interest in the individuals associated with the vessels past and present, and his pleasure in a 'good crack' along with the work, were well known and greatly appreciated. Thus it is that so many people have delighted in assisting him with details for this book, making it a rich and vibrant record of lives lived in a maritime milieu. They could have had no more sympathetic or enthusiastic chronicler than this, adopted Scot.

In compiling this volume Walter Weyndling has made a unique and invaluable contribution to Scotland's ethnological record, performing a much needed service by drawing together information from diverse sources in a permanent form. Importantly, he has ensured that those whose lives and experience have been so closely bound up with the ferries of the west are not forgotten but are given an honoured place and a lasting voice in our history. Students, scholars, natives of the localities described and readers interested in Scotland and beyond, including those undertaking comparative studies of maritime communities, will be grateful now and in the future for this painstaking work of documentation and commemoration.

Another of the Gaelic bards of the west, Donald MacIntyre of Paisley and South Uist (1889–1964), known as Dòmhnall Ruadh, captured in song the anticipation and the pleasure that a ferry voyage to a loved destination could provide. The celebratory spirit expressed in the following verse[1] surely matches the welcome this book will receive from all with an interest in Scotland's maritime history.

> Nuair ruigeas mi 'n cidhe cha bhi mi fo ghruaimean,
> Coinnichidh a fichead a thig o'n taobh tuath mi;
> 'Tha thu air tilleadh a Mhic Aonghais Ruaidh;
> Nach tiugainn sinn suas gum faigheamaid stòp.'

> When I get to the pier I shall not be gloomy,
> Twenty will meet me, from the north;
> 'You've come back, son of Angus Ruadh;
> Come on up and we'll get a dram.'

Margaret A. Mackay
School of Scottish Studies, University of Edinburgh
Spring 1996

---

1 *Sporan Dhòmhnaill*, ed. Somerled MacMillan, Edinburgh: Scottish Gaelic Texts Society, 1968, p. 9.

PREFACE

A chiel's amang you, taking notes,
And, faith, he'll prent it.

Robert Burns

In Argyll the land is vast and the people thin on the ground. And yet those who sail her waters and work her boats know all about one another. They form a sort of far-flung parish in which a marine surveyor could take up a role in some ways akin to that of a minister. A willing surveyor or 'Mr Board of Trade' was not quite the man from the ministry but rather a guardian of the boatmens' safety, a father confessor, a wise uncle and a chum rolled into one. Working with and observing ferries and ferrymen and listening to their tales led me to taking notes. In time I began to feel that a permanent record might be worthwhile. That in turn made me look for more people with ferry tales to tell and to delve into history. The resulting book has its limitations, of course.

Such sources as I was able to tap did not, on the whole, take me much further back than the eighteenth century. But the era of the regular ferries between the islands and the Argyll mainland dawned towards the end of the fifteenth century in consequence of the centre of political gravity having shifted from the islands with the demise of the Lordship of the Isles. From then on the islands tended to be controlled from Inveraray which gave rise to a system of communication between them and the mainland. The importance of the ferries grew in the seventeenth century when the opening of the English cattle markets called for more cattle to be ferried. In addition, the reformed kirk wanted all islanders to be able to attend on Sundays.

The 1909 County Council List of Ferries in Argyll names thirty which were functioning at the time. This book refers to twenty-five of them and to several others. It took most of my working life on the West Coast of Scotland, and some years beyond it, to gather the 'tales' that make up this book. I have now realised that my life is unlikely to be long enough to tell of all the Argyll ferries!

In Chapter 13 I travelled well beyond the boundaries of the present mainland District of Argyll. My reason for doing so is due partly to the historical extent of Argyll and partly to the complex geography of that part of the West Coast. Arran and Bute are also outside the boundaries of Argyll but they are among the 'Isles', and I have enjoyed a close association with both.

Walter Weyndling

ACKNOWLEDGEMENTS

This book is dedicated to the people, mostly from Argyll, whose generous help and contributions made the writing of this book possible, and whose names appear below, and to those I have inadvertently omitted. They helped in a variety of ways, telling tales, allowing me to use their historical research or anecdotal material, lending photographs and drawings and giving support of every kind. I would especially like to thank Dr Mairi MacArthur for allowing me to use extracts from her books.

The late Jim Aikman-Smith of Edinburgh; David Aris of Oxenholme, Cumbria; Mrs Jean Baker of Easdale; Mrs Ian Beaton of Kerrera; George Bergius of Lochgilphead; Richard Blair of Long Itchington, Warwickshire; Duncan Cameron of Scarinish, Tiree; Alaistair Campbell of Airds, of Invrawe; the late Miss Marion Campbell of Kilberry; the late Roni Cameron from Lochaline; Mr and Mrs E. Clark of Tarbett; Jimmy Cowie of Ardrossan; Mrs I. Crawford of Loch Awe; Miss Flora Currie of Pirnmill, Arran; the late Donald Darroch of Feolin, Jura; Dr Jane Dawson of Edinburgh; Arthur Galbraith of Toberonachy, Luing; Mrs Hilary Giles of Tarbett; Gordon Grant of Iona; John Green of Perth; Dr Arthur Kitchin of Edinburgh; Donald Lawrie of Lochaline; the late Dr W.D. Lamont of Glasgow; Bryce Leitch of Larkhall, Lanarkshire; Sir William Lithgow of Ormsary; the late Robert Logan of Corrie, Arran; John MacAllister of Seil; Mrs Jean MacArthur of Inveraray; the late Dougald MacArthur of Oban; Dr Mairi MacArthur of Strathpeffer; the late Mrs Mary MacArthur of Port Appin; the late Mr and Mrs Neil MacArthur of Iona; Graham MacCulloch of Gigha; Alan Macdonald from Glenuig; the late Capt. Colin Macdonald of Iona; Hugh Macdonald of Lochaline; Ian Macdonald of Clachan; Murdo MacDonald of Lochgilphead; the late Duncan MacDougall of Tarbert; Duncan MacDougall of Tarbert; the late Miss Hope MacDougall of MacDougall, of Oban; Lawrence MacDuff of Glasgow; Duncan MacEachen of Kerrera; Finlay MacFadyean of Colonsay; Mrs Rae MacGregor of Inveraray; Lady M. McGrigor of Dalmally; Dr Margaret Mackay of Edinburgh; the late Donald MacKechnie of Inveraray; the late Ian and Flora McKechnie of Tayinloan; Brig. John Macfarlane of Taynuilt; the late Miss Anne Macfarlane from Taynuilt; Mrs Sheila MacIntyre of Inveraray; Donald MacKinnon of Sandaig, Tiree; Lachie MacKinnon of Kilchrenan; the late John Mackenzie of Oban; the late Lachlan MacLachlan and Mrs Jane MacLachlan of Cullipool, Luing; Hugh Maclean of Barropol, Tiree; the late Charlie Maclean of Jura; Mrs Macleod of Achleek, Loch Sunnart; Campbell MacMurray from Campbeltown; Miss Betty MacNeill of Gigha; Donald 'Gibby' MacNeill of Colonsay; Mrs Kathie MacNeill of Scarinish, Tiree; the late Archie MacPhee of Port Askaig, Islay; Donald and Bella MacQueen of Oban; Seamus MacSporran from Gigha; Angus Mathew of Kilchrenan; Prof. Donald Meek from Tiree; the late Capt. Edward Rankine of Arran; Hugh Raven of Kinlochalin; Capt. and Mrs William Robertson from Tobermory; Douglas Rolland of Kilmichael Glassary; Mrs Gela Rose of Kilchrenan; the late Hugh Ross of North Shian; the late Capt. Alaistair Sillars of Arran; Ian Scott of Port Bannatyne, Bute; Norman Tait of Renfrew; Duncan Thomson of Dunmore, Whitehouse; Miss Janet Thomson from Port Appin; Ian Thornber of Lochaline; Jack Wallace of Catacol, Arran; Tony Whelan of Rothesay, Bute; the present and past directors of Western Ferries of Glasgow; Peter Wordie of Glasgow.

However, it is Dr Margaret Mackay, the Director of the School of Scottish Studies in Edinburgh, and Campbell MacMurray, the then Director of the Royal Naval Museum in Portsmouth and formerly Director of the Scottish Maritime Museum, to whom I owe a special debt of gratitude for having inspired and encouraged the publication of this book.

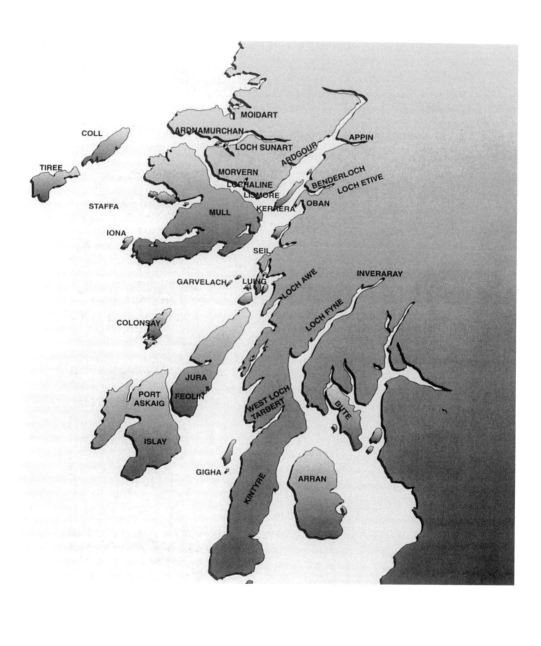

1

ARRAN

The Isle of Arran has no natural all-weather harbours, but Lochranza in the north and Brodick and Lamlash bays in the east provide relatively sheltered ports of call and good anchorages.

The first record of an Arran ferry I have been able to find relates to a sailing/rowing ferry established in 1684 to ply between Lochranza and 'Dungavie' (probably Dunagoil on the Isle of Bute – see Chapter 2). It could not have been a paying proposition, for it did not survive for long.

An advertisement in the *Glasgow Journal* of March 1759 informed readers that 'a packet boat was to pass every week from Arran to Saltcoats on the Ayrshire Coast for the convenience of travellers', and that 'freight was fixed to prevent impositions'. This enterprise probably met the same fate as the earlier one.

Eleven years later, almost to the day, an advertisement was read out in the churches of Arran giving notice that a meeting of the island's tenants and heritors was to be held at Cladoch in order to 'consider the establishment of a packet boat for the service to the island'. A vote was taken to decide on the mainland terminal, and Saltcoats was chosen in preference to Ayr. The list of those attending seems quite impressive: John Burrell, the estate commissioner; George Cooper, the estate factor; William MacGregor, overseer to the Duke of Hamilton; two ministers; a surgeon; an officer of excise; and eight tenant representatives. The commissioner's suggestion that no islander should pay freight was accepted. All were to assess their own contribution for the upkeep of the ferry in proportion to their rent or to 'their souming or sowing'. The duke was to provide the sailing packet, and until one could be built to his order, a vessel was hired and began weekly crossings to Saltcoats.

By November 1770, there were two packet-boats running, one from Brodick to Saltcoats with Hans Bannatyne as master, another from Imachar on the west coast of Arran, presumably to Grogport or Carradale on the Kintyre peninsula, commanded by Duncan Sillar. From then on, travellers could plan their journeys according to the packets' schedules, but only to the nearest week, rather than the nearest day.

John Burrell, the estate commissioner, recorded how, in July 1772, he arrived at Saltcoats to find the packet had been there the previous afternoon but was gone. He went on to Ayr, where he found the packet on call, but there was no wind, and he could not leave Ayr until 2 a.m. on the following day, reaching Brodick eight hours later. Evidently, someone had a grudge against the packet, or the ducal representative, for in January 1773, when the commissioner was about to leave for the mainland, the rudder was found to be broken and 2 ft of planking had been cut out of the starboard side.

In 1776, a new boat was commissioned, specially built of fir and oak cut in the castle grounds and costing £94 3s 3d. There was a crew of three, including Hans Bannatyne, the skipper. It is sad to recall that in May 1776, long before the construction of the ferry had been paid for, Hans Bannatyne, his eldest son, and another lad by the name of Fullerton were all drowned when the ferry capsized while crossing with some cattle.

In the first quarter of the nineteenth century, Arran was reputed to be something of a health resort, and its goat's milk was renowned for its curative properties. However, the nature of ferrying of that period could turn any therapeutic holiday into an adventure. A report from Ayr in the *Glasgow Herald* of 9 July 1824 read:

> Last night a fleet of boats from Arran, equal to the navy of the Sandwich Isles, arrived here, crowded with passengers, potatoes, poultry, pigs, pipers, plaiden, eggs and yarn, to attend our midsummer fair. In the hurry and bustle of landing some of the hardy islanders fell into the water, to the great amusement of the vast concourse of people assembled to witness their arrival.

By the 1820s, a regular steamer service was established between the east coast of Arran and the mainland. A steam packet ran twice a week to Ardrossan in the winter and spring months, and daily in the summer, with an additional service run by another company from June to September. However, the south and west of Arran were still served by the old-fashioned sailing packets; one ran from Southend to Ayr and another from Blackwaterfoot to Campbeltown, each subsidised by the tenantry paying a sum in addition to their rent.

As long as the ferries depended on the wind, passengers had to reckon with a very elastic timetable. In one of the years when steam was 'making straight the crooked highways of the wind', a young lady left Brodick on a December morning to go to Glasgow for the New Year. The smack drifted leisurely along under a breath of wind, and by dark it was abreast of Saltcoats. The passengers had to spend the night on board. A passenger's herrings and the sailors' potatoes boiled in seawater were their fare. Next morning, a steamer toiling up from Ayr towed them into the Clyde. There, another night was spent in a riverside inn, and at last their destination was reached on the third morning. However, such adventures were becoming a rarity with the rapid proliferation of Clyde steamers.

From an 1829 advertisement it appears that the *Toward Castle* sailed from Glasgow to Brodick and Lamlash every Tuesday, returning on Wednesday, and

Sketch of the ferry cottage at Pirnmill (by the author)

the *Inveraray Castle* sailed every Saturday, returning from Arran on Monday. From 1832 to 1846, the McKellar steamers, the *Hero,* the *Jupiter* and the *Juno,* were familiar on the Arran route. In 1868, the Duke of Hamilton once again entered the trade with *Lady Mary.* In 1870, Captain William Buchanan came onto the Arran ferry scene with the *Rothesay Castle.*

The last of the sailing packets to carry mail and cattle between Brodick and Ardrossan was the *Brodick,* built by Fyfe's of Fairlie in 1832 as a sloop and later converted to a schooner. She was skippered by James Hamilton, whose son, Adam, and grandsons, George and Gavin, were founders of the Cloy Line. The first puffer of that line, destined for the steam trade between Arran and the mainland, was the *Glencoy,* built in 1895 in a field at Low Glencoy on Arran, of local timber. She was followed by the *Invercloy* and the *River Cloy.* Some Hay Line puffers named after nationalities were also involved in ferrying to and from Arran. One of them, the *Roman,* ended her days owned by an Arran syndicate. In 1957, she sailed out of Corrie to be broken up.

Until well into the second half of the nineteenth century, Arran suffered from the absence of piers, and ferries as well as cruise steamers had to rely on small ferry boats to shuttle between the ship and the shore. In 1872, a steamer pier was built at Brodick, and in 1885 one was built at Lochranza. In the late 1870s, William Buchanan's *Scotia* and his Arran ferry enterprise passed to the Glasgow & Southwestern Railway Company, whose *Glen Sannox* succeeded

The *Fairy Dell* unloading at Lochranza (loaned by Mrs Jean Kinloch)

the *Scotia*. In 1890, the Caledonian Steam Packet Company doubled the Arran ferry trade with the *Duchess of Hamilton*. In 1901, when the Wemyss Bay pier was completed, her route was extended to that pier.

While the steamers' principal ports of call were the island's piers at Brodick, Lochranza, and later at Lamlash and Whiting Bay, small ferries continued to be used to carry passengers and cargo between the steamers and the intermediate coastal villages, such as Pirnmill on the west side and Corrie on the east side, well into the twentieth century.

At Pirnmill, a rowing boat served ships leaving or approaching Lochranza from the early years of the Campbeltown steamer service. At the end of the nineteenth century, the Pirnmill ferryman was a Mr Cook, and in 1920, his son-in-law, Charles Robertson, was running a big rowing ferry. The ferry cottage built by Mr Cook stands on the main road, a little to the south of the jetty: the recent sketch shows that it has been well maintained. The Pirnmill ferry jetty was built by voluntary labour in 1930; prior to that, a gangway on iron wheels was used for passenger access between the beach and the boat.

Archie Currie took over as Pirnmill ferryman a little before the Second World War. He had three boats: two big rowing boats and one 24-ft ex-ship's lifeboat with a 7.9 h.p. petrol/paraffin engine and a lug sail. Archie's daughter, Miss Flora Currie of Pirnmill, remembers the twice-daily arrivals of the ferry as the highlights of the day. The ships the Currie ferries served were the Campbeltown and Glasgow Steamship Company's *Davaar* and *Dalriada*.

The steamer *Davaar* off Pirnmill (loaned by Jack Wallace)

The ferries had to pick up cargo and passengers from the passing steamers, the cargo being anything from cement to live calves. Most cargo came from Glasgow, so its time of arrival was known, and therefore when the wind was strong and from a southerly direction, the ferry would go northwards to meet the ship leaving Lochranza and was towed back. Some of the cargo had to be handled rapidly, such as blocks of ice wrapped in hessian. Some did not need a ferry, such as horses from Tarbert Fair, which swam ashore. Some deliveries to the ships from the ferries used to be undertaken by boys running along the steamer belting; at least that is how bottles of whisky – at 12s 6d each – were sneaked in for the engineers' benefit, Lochranza and Pirnmill being 'dry'. Flora Currie remembers how young men and boys on holiday in Pirnmill used to help her father to man the sweeps (long oars). Many a boy's ambition was to be allowed to use a sweep on the ferry.

During the Second World War, Campbeltown steamers were withdrawn from service, but Archie Currie kept up the service between the west coast of Arran and the Kintyre peninsula, carrying passengers from Pirnmill to Carradale; the crossing took sixty minutes. The ferry also carried parcels of cargo and passengers' bicycles. There were day trips, wind and weather permitting, often connecting with the Carradale–Campbeltown bus, allowing a day's shopping in Campbeltown. The photograph of one such day trip in the 1940s was kindly given by Miss Flora Currie. There was an annual crossing to collect shepherds and dogs from Kintyre for the Pirnmill and Machrie Sheepdog Trials. It is said that at one time there were other shore-to-ship ferries on the west side, from Machrie and Blackwaterfoot, but they did not survive as long as the Pirnmill ferry.

A postcard showing a ferry being boarded at Pirnmill (loaned by Jack Wallace)

At least until the Second World War, on the east side of the island, at Corrie, a ferry met the cruise steamers out of Gourock which called at piers in the Kyles of Bute and then at Brodick, Lamlash and Whiting Bay, returning via Garroch Head. Early in the twentieth century, such distinguished steamers as the *Duchess of Argyll, Duchess of Fife,* and *Duchess of Rothesay* and such distinguished skippers as Captain Macnaughton operated that cruise route. Between the wars, the ferry – a rowing boat of about 30 ft in length – was run from Ferry Rock at the north end of Corrie by Tom Kelso until his death in 1928, and from then until September 1939 by Captain Robert Kelso, who was previously master of the Clyde and Campbeltown Shipping Company cargo vessel *Bute.* There were two ferry boats at Corrie at this time, one for passengers and one for luggage only, the latter being called into use at the beginning and end of the summer months, and also, of course, at the beginning and end of the Glasgow Fair holiday (the last two weeks of July). The record number of passengers carried by the Corrie ferry was 102 on a calm day.

Corrie's Ferry Rock is pockmarked, as it was blasted piecemeal to form a landing stage. Willie Macmillan Stewart of Corrie tells of a conversation between Colonel Laird, a regular visitor to Arran, and Robert King, known locally as a bit of a wag. Colonel Laird informed Robert that it was his father who was instrumental in shaping the Ferry Rock. 'Aye, I thought so,' said Robert, 'he left his teeth marks on it.'

Since the Second World War, calls at Arran piers by Clyde and Campbeltown cruising ships became less frequent and gradually came to an end, except for the resuscitated paddlesteamer *Waverley.* The shore-to-ship ferry boats therefore lost their *raison d'être.*

Archie Currie's ferry (loaned by Miss Flora Currie)

On the east side of Arran, car ferries were introduced on the Fairlie–Ardrossan run as early as 1954. The one that stands out in my memory is the *Caledonia*. She started life in the Baltic as the *Stena Baltica* and was bought for the new Ardrossan–Brodick run in 1960. She was brought over from Scandinavia in 1970 by Alec Ferrier, who became her mate and later her master. From then on, as far as Alec was concerned, the name of *Caledonia* was sacrosanct next only to that of Glasgow Rangers.

Alec Ferrier and I (in my capacity as Board of Trade Surveyor) crawled through every nook and cranny of that ship and packed her with fire protection and every safety device, in accordance with latest requirements, before a passenger certificate was granted. In the end, she had just enough stability to meet the rules, but not much more, and she was still fairly 'tender', tending to heel over when turning, etc.

Next winter, a relief master was in command on a day when a north-westerly gale was hurtling down the Firth of Clyde. He did what would have been prudent with most ships, but not with the *Caledonia*: he sailed her into the wind in order to turn in the lee of the Isle of Bute to begin the run downwind to Ardrossan. The turning heel of the ship, added to the heel caused by the wind on her beam, produced an angle of 17°. The ship righted herself and came to no harm, but a cattle truck overturned on the car deck, and sheep rejoicing in their newly regained freedom ran all over the deck, which alarmed the passengers somewhat.

Caledonia at Broddick pier, Isle of Arran

That night, there were phone calls from the press, and I had an uphill struggle to put the matter into perspective. In the end, the pressure of public opinion on Arran, perhaps stirred up by the press, was such that a fair amount of additional ballast had to be put into the ship's bottom, and this reduced her carrying capacity to about 70 tons. Eventually, that led to her being relegated, for the summer at least, to the Oban–Craignure (on Mull) run where carrying capacity was not so critical, and the lengthened *Clansman* replaced her on the Ardrossan–Brodick run. *Caledonian Isles*, which can carry 120 cars, is the ferry on this run at the time of writing.

Alec Ferrier remained in command of the Ardrossan–Brodick ferry until his untimely death in harness. He was one of the most dedicated, and certainly most popular, of the Arran ferrymasters. A bollard at Brodick pier clearly marked 'Ferrier's Bollard' is a visible testimony to the affection in which he was generally held.

The summer-only west-side ferry crossing is from Claonaig near Skipness, just off the Tarbert-Carradale road on the Kintyre peninsula, to Lochranza. The service started with the *Kilbrannan,* a 68-ft steel car ferry of the 'Scottish Islands' class, built in 1972 at James Lamont's shipyard in Port Glasgow, the first 'landing-craft' type of ferry run by Caledonian Macbrayne. She was capable of carrying five cars. The original rota of skippers included Jim Andrews, a retired deep-sea captain, and two well-known Clyde passenger ferrymasters, Callum Morrison, previously in command on the small Gourock-Kilcreggan ferry, and Duncan Macdonald of the small Rhubodach-

Colintraive ferry in the Kyles of Bute (see Chapter 2). Duncan and Callum were used to grounding on the shore at the end of each half-hour passage, but for a deep-sea master like Jim, it went against the grain at first, and he was more likely to cancel crossings on account of the weather. There was a notable accident in 1980, when a car drove off the ferry into the sea. Fortunately the driver was saved from drowning by a local fisherman.

In 1973, it became necessary to improve on the *Kilbrannan* by substituting the *Rhum,* a 74-ft ferry carrying seven cars, with a better drive for the hydraulic unit activating the bow ramp. By 1988, increasing traffic demanded the introduction of the much bigger, 100-ft long, *Lochranza,* capable of transporting twelve cars.

At the time of writing the even bigger *Loch Tarbert* links Arran with Kintyre. For many years the ferry has been skippered by a Box & Cox arrangement, helmed in turn by Jimmy Cowie and Jackie Wallace, two very versatile and experienced men. Since Jackie's retirement the same arrangement continues with young Donald MacKelvie having taken Jackie's place. The old pier at Lochranza is in the process of being restored which will allow the ferry to lie alongside and will put an end to the crew's late night and early morning escapades by dinghy while the ship is at a mooring.

2

BUTE

The Isle of Bute forms a long, narrow barrier between the Firth of Clyde and the mouth of Loch Fyne. Its northern end is tucked into a chink in Argyll's Cowal Peninsula. Its southern end looks south-west over Arran and east to the Ayrshire coast and the Cumbrae islands, together with which it protects the upper reaches of the Firth of Clyde from the worst of the south-westerly gales.

The earliest record of Bute ferries I could find dates from 1680, when the heritors (parish landholders) of Bute appointed Donald MacFie to be ferryman of Scoulag, on the east side of the island, opposite Largs on the Ayrshire mainland. The appointment carried the usual privileges. No others were to be allowed to carry persons on that station, on condition 'that he should always be prepared to afford victuals, drink and lodgings for strangers waiting at the ferry'. No particular proprietor had a right to this ferry by charter, and the management devolved solely on the family of Bute.

A short time later, in 1684, a ferry was established from 'Dungarie' (probably Dunagoil Bay on Bute's south-western shore) to Lochranza on Arran. The ferryman was allowed 36s Scots every voyage.[1] He was required to have a boat well furnished with a mast, sails, four oars and other equipment, to provide passengers with meat and drink, a fire and lodgings for a reasonable charge, and, among other provisions, to have aqua vitae, or brandy, available at all times. This service did not become as firmly established as the Largs one, and in time the ferry to neighbouring Arran was routed via Ayrshire, as it is today. However, some vestige of a direct ferry service might have remained until the early part of the nineteenth century, because the 1820 *Lumsden's Steamboat Companion* mentions that you might get a boat to Arran from the south-western shore of Bute.

Until 1799, a sailing vessel was employed to carry the island's mail between Rothesay and Greenock three times a week. When the boat's two sailors demanded a rise on their £11 5s annual payment, it was decided that the mail could be conveyed more economically and speedily on the Scoulag-Largs ferry. This system continued until the steamer service took over.

---

1 For an explanation of Scots currency, see the Glossary, under 'pound Scots'.

Kerrycroy pier (loaned by Dr Arthur Kitchin)

The Scoulag-Largs sailing/rowing ferry survived until 1804/5. At that time, the Bute Estate extended the policies of Mount Stuart northwards and moved the ferry quay to Kerrycroy, a model village built about a mile to the north and west of Scoulag. The ferry from Kerrycroy pier to a beach at Largs continued until 1830.

There is no trace of the pier at Scoulag Point today, only the remains of an elaborate 70-ft long boathouse. This might have been intended for the *Lady Guildford,* 32 ft long, 8 ft in beam, with three masts, twelve oars and described as a 'lugger'. She was built between 1817 and 1819 at Tighnabruaich for the 2nd Marquess of Bute, to bring his bride, Lady Maria, daughter of the Earl of Guildford, to the island. The *Lady Guildford* was used by the Bute family as a ferry to the mainland, and remained afloat until 1939, to be later relegated to Peter MacIntyre's boatyard at Port Bannatyre. She is now in the Scottish Maritime Museum at Irvine.

The place-name of Ascog, some 1½ miles north of Kerrycroy, may suggest that there was a ferry there at one time.[2] It still has a stone pier, which in more recent days might have been used in connection with the salt pans there, and also as a bad-weather ferry terminal, Ascog Bay being sheltered from the south.

From Ardbeg, about 1¼ miles north of Rothesay, another ferry used to run to Ardyne Point on Cowal. Although an arduous walk lay before them, this was the shortest route for travellers to Dunoon. It has been said that this

---

2 The Gaelic for 'ferry' is *aiseag.* Norse settlers hardened the 'sh' sound to 'sk', giving rise to place-names such as Ascog and Askaig. (See Glossary)

The boathouse at Scoulag Point (loaned by Dr Arthur Kitchin)

was the route favoured by pedlars from the mainland looking for business on Bute.

Regular steamer services between Rothesay (where Bute's first steamer pier was built), Greenock and Gourock began in 1815, gradually replacing not only the sailing packets between those ports, but also the Kerrycroy–Largs ferry. Royal Mail carried by the ferry was transferred to the steamers in 1825. While the ferry was subject to supervision by the justices of the peace, the Commission of Supply's supervision of the sailing packets, and later of the steamers replacing them, was at best very tenuous.

The second steamer pier on Bute was not built until the 1880s. Situated at Kilchatten Bay, it was intended to serve the south of the island. Prior to that, steamer passengers for Kilchatten were landed there by a rowing ferry. The pier remained in use until 1955.

The most natural ferry crossing between Bute and the mainland is across the 400 yards of the East Kyle of Bute, between Rhubodach ('Old Man's Point') on the island side of Colintraive (Caol-an-t'snàimh, 'Narrows of the Swimming') on Cowal. For a long time, the crossing was of special importance for swimming cattle from Cowal across the Rhubodach tide-rip, particularly for St Blain's market. Cattle sold at that market were driven to Glencallum Bay, at the southern end of the island, from where a boat ferried them to Ardrossan on the Ayrshire coast. It appears that the relatively less important passenger trade was a free-for-all among small ferry operators.

The Bute Ferry Company was formed by the Bute family in modern times, and their first vehicular ferries started their regular Kyles of Bute service in about 1950. The *Eilean Mhor* was a 52-ft long, single-ended, wooden landing-craft capable of carrying four cars, and the *Eilean Fraioch,* a smaller craft of similar type, could carry two cars. Their arrival did not stop local independent boatmen making casual ferry crossings of the Kyles of Bute narrows. One such was Archibald Clark, a Colintraive boat-hirer. Ian Morris of Colintraive remembered being ferried by Archie Clark in his small open motorboat in the early hours of a summer morning in 1947, together with his two mates and three bicycles. In the 1950s he ran a small, steel landing craft called the *Jura* as his freelance ferry.

On the night of 19 May 1956, Archie Clark was due to convey from Rhubodach to Colintraive some twenty-five Argyll shinty players, who had won the 'Buteman' Cup at the Rothesay Meadows Cup Final. It so happened that the ferryman had had a jolly evening in the Colintraive Hotel while waiting for a phone call from his passengers.

When the victorious team embarked at Rhubodach at about 11 p.m., the *Jura's* engine would not start. In the end, Archie improvised a tow by lashing a motorboat to the craft, but when he at last got going, he omitted to raise the *Jura's* bow ramp above the waterline. The ferry was swamped in no time, and everyone finished up in the water or scrambling on to the towing motorboat. Fortunately, the weather and the sea were calm, and in spite of darkness, all but one on board were rescued. The passenger who drowned was a respected Cowal farmer.

In due course, the ferryman was tried and sentenced, and the local Board of Trade marine surveyors woke up to the fact that there was not one vessel among the Kyles ferry fleet which could boast a passenger certificate. Because I was relatively unknown, being the newest surveyor in Greenock, having arrived there from Glasgow in 1959, I was dispatched to Colintraive as it was thought that my arrival at Colintraive would not arouse suspicion. The efficiency of the bush telegraph was underestimated.

I turned up at Colintraive pier accompanied by my wife and a pram containing my newborn offspring. Little did those innocents know that they were destined to witness history in the making. The ferry skipper was to be caught red-handed carrying more than twelve passengers without a certificate. I stepped on board with my unsuspecting entourage after some twenty-five passengers had embarked. My intention was to utter the time-honoured caution, 'anything you say . . .' before the vessel reached mid-channel, so that the ensuing prosecution would take place in Argyll Sheriff Court, to avoid embarrassing the Marquess of Bute, as head of the Bute Ferry Company, by arraigning him before the Sheriff of Bute. But the best laid plans of mice and men . . .

Before I had time to utter the caution, Duncan Macdonald, the ferrymaster, came up to me with outstretched hand: 'Welcome on board, Mr Surveyor. I

The *Eilean Buidhe* on trials. Her designers are on the right, with her builder and surveyor on the left

expected your visit, and I think I know what you are going to say.' By the time the exchange of pleasantries came to an end, the ferry was well past mid-channel and safely within Bute Sheriff Court's jurisdiction. The court let the marquess off with a warning but exacted from him a promise that the Bute Ferry Company would commission the construction of a new ferry, purpose-built under the Board of Trade's supervision. His lordship expressed preference for timber construction, so that his own estates could provide the building material.

The contract for the new Bute ferry was entrusted to Dickie's of Tarbert, Loch Fyne, known as builders of small, wooden fishing boats, and the design to Alfred Mylne & Company, well-known yacht designers. The hull was built largely of plywood (whether made from Bute Estate's timber it would have been tactless to ask), was double-ended and had a long overhang at each end. The vessel was named the *Eilean Buidhe* after one of the islands in the Kyles of Bute, carried six cars and was powered by twin diesel engines turning continuous shafts driving propellers at each end of the boat. When she was completed in 1963, the marquess invited all concerned to a slap-up lunch at

The *Eilean Buidhe* at Tarbert where she was built

his Glenburn Hotel in Rothesay, after which the commissioning ceremony
was to take place at Rhubodach.

The cavalcade of cars processing up the Kyles was headed by the marquess's
Mercedes, followed by a similar vehicle carrying the Bute children in the
charge of the Bute nanny, and then by lesser conveyances. Just as the
Mercedes proceeded up the ferry ramp to break the ceremonial ribbon, there
was a loud crunch as its exhaust grounded on the ramp.

From that ominous start onwards, nothing went right with the *Eilean
Buidhe*, which was locally named *The White Ghost*. The weight of the lorries
carried on the overhanging decks caused the timber structure to hog (arch)
by inches, which in turn made the long, continuous propeller shafts seize in
the bearings.

After protracted deliberations, it was decided that the propeller shafts
should be replaced by two diesel-driven water jets. The jets, produced by
Thames Ironworks, were duly installed in 1964, and the new system impressed
all with its simplicity and ingenuity. Whichever happened to be the forward
jet was effectively used for propulsion and the after jet for steering. The only
snag was that the speed of the ferry produced by this mechanism was barely
sufficient to maintain steerageway, let alone to cope with the full tide-rip of
the Kyle narrows.

Having invested in a purpose-built ferry for six cars, the Bute Ferry Company had to fall back on the old, wooden, four-car *Eilean Mhor,* limited to twelve passengers, supplemented by another four-car, wooden landing-craft, the *Eilean Dhu,* acquired in 1965, for which a passenger certificate was granted after a survey and modifications. In 1967, the company bought the *Dhuirinish,* a ferry which had served on the crossing at Kessock, near Inverness. It was of similar dimensions to the other two, but built of steel, and it carried six cars.

Two years later, the Bute fleet of the *Eilean Buidhe, Eilean Dhu* and *Dhuirinish* was taken over by the Caledonian Steam Packet Company, and the poor *Eilean Buidhe* never sailed again. The new owners brought the steel ferries *Portree* and *Broadford* from Kyle of Lochalsh in 1970/1. They were of the side-loading type, and had to be rebuilt and re-equipped with double-hinging bow ramps. They served until 1986, when the *Loch Riddon,* one of the four 'Loch' class boats built at Hessle on Humberside, was introduced. More than twice the length of the original Bute ferries, she carries twelve cars, is double-ended and has double-hinged ramps to ensure watertight bow and stern closures.

The other short ferry crossing (three-quarters of a mile) joining Bute to the Argyll mainland crossed the West Kyles, running between Blair's Ferry on the Ardlamont peninsula, about a mile south of Kames on the coast road to Ardlamont Point, and Ferry Port on Bute, about half a mile south of Kilmichael Farm on the north-west of the island. The rowing ferry used to come into a cleft in the rocks on the Bute side, protected by a stone breakwater built in 1769. On the Ardlamont side, Blair's Ferry had a stone pier. Originally, the service was run from the Bute side, where the ferry house and inn stands to this day, now uninhabited, hidden by trees, off the road to Kilmichael. More recently, it was run from Blair's Ferry, where the ferry house also still stands intact.

The first record I have found of Blair's ferry dates from 1700, when a complaint was lodged with Rothesay Kirk accusing the ferryman of operating on the Sabbath. Stories are told that this isolated ferry was well suited to trading in whisky illicitly distilled somewhere in Argyll and smuggled in sheep's bladders secreted under women's voluminous petticoats.

In the late nineteenth century, young lads from the Kames district of Ardlamont travelled by this ferry to attend what must have been a very early 'further education' class on the island. Once on Bute, they had to walk five miles to Port Bannatyne, where the headmaster of the local school taught the rudiments of navigation.

Blair's ferry continued until the Second World War, although Mr Ritchie, the Rothesay fishmonger, thinks the service was carried on for some time after this by Councillor Shaw of Kames.

3
COLONSAY

Colonsay is a small island (together with its even smaller partner, Oronsay, only twenty-three square miles in area). It lies between the Ross of Mull and the Islay/Jura group, but considerably closer to the latter. That is why, from the earliest times, Colonsay relied primarily on ferry links with Islay and Jura for passenger and cattle transport, although clan politics seem to have played some part in shaping this relationship.

The earliest story I have found relating to ferries to and from Colonsay is a remarkable one quoted in John de Vere Loder's *Colonsay and Oronsay*. It seeks to account for the settlement of a branch of the Clan Neill in Colonsay around the period of the break-up of the Lordship of the Isles, towards the end of the fifteenth and the beginning of the sixteenth centuries.

The wives of Macduffie of Colonsay and Macneill of Barra were both pregnant and arrangements were made for the exchange of the infants (this was a common practice at the time, designed to cement peaceful relations between clans). Macneill's wife was to be ferried to Colonsay for the confinement.

The journey in a small boat would have been trying in the best of weather, but it was winter. A storm arose, and it began to snow, when the Macneill lady was seized with the pains of labour, and a child was born while the ferry was still some way from Colonsay.

The mother and the child might have died from exposure had the crew not had an inspiration. The cow on board was killed and gralloched (gutted) and the mother and the baby were placed in the warm carcass, where they remained until they were safely brought to land the same evening. Ian a Chain ('John of the Ocean'), as the child came to be called, was brought up on Colonsay.

Another account in Loder's book of the difficulties of relying on a ferry to and from Colonsay refers to the complaints addressed to his presbytery by the minister of the parish of Jura and Colonsay at the turn of the eighteenth century.

Mr Donald MacNicol of Jura claimed an increase in his stipend of £139 6s 9d, of which £50 had to be paid yearly to an assistant serving Colonsay, largely because the cost of ferry travel exceeded the allowance: 'He begs leave to state that the Sacrament is alternatively administered in the distant island of Colonsay, belonging to his parish, the access to which is difficult and expensive, having nine miles to travel by land and then a dangerous ferry of upwards of twenty miles to cross.'

From the mileages given, we can try to determine which ferry crossing the assistant minister used. The most likely harbour on Jura which would be suitable for a ferry and over twenty miles from Scalasaig on Colonsay is Kinuachdrach on the north-east coast of Jura, and the only starting point on Jura about nine miles by road from Kinuachdrach is Inverlussa/Lussagiven. It is known that Kinuachdrach had a relatively sizeable population for most of the nineteenth century and that it was one of the destinations of the Colonsay cattle ferry, being convenient for trans-shipment to Craignish on the mainland. Inverlussa/Lussagiven might have had a reasonable population before the clearances, but would an assistant minister have had his base there? Considering an alternative, the shortest, and therefore most obvious, crossing to Jura from Scalasaig is to the Loch Tarbert jetty, to which a road was built at the beginning of the nineteenth century, but the length of the sea passage would, at eleven miles, be only about half that quoted, although the nine miles from the Loch Tarbert jetty to the chapel at Craighouse would fit the land mileage stated.

The present stone harbour wall and the stone slip at Scalasaig, the 'capital' of Colonsay, were built by John MacNeill, 'the old laird', in the first half of the nineteenth century. Lord Teignmouth praised the harbour in Colonsay when he wrote in 1836 that it was the best in the Hebrides for repairing inter-island vessels. Prior to the construction of the breakwater and slip, a rock to the south of the present slip was used for embarkation and disembarkation. The passenger traffic went mainly to Islay, whose nearest point would be Rubha' a'Mhàil, eight miles from Scalasaig, but the nearest harbour would be Port Askaig in the Sound of Islay, some fourteen miles from Scalasaig. The cattle traffic went either to Port Askaig to be ferried to Jura, then following the drove route across Jura, or to Loch Tarbert jetty on the west side of Jura, or else directly to Kinuachdrach Harbour on the north-east coast of Jura. In either case, the cattle would end up being driven to Loch Awe, and from there to the Dalmally cattle sales (see Chapter 10).

For a long time, the principal means of transport between Colonsay and the mainland was a sailing packet-boat. A communal one was bought for £200 in 1767. It carried passengers, mail and freight, and it plied between Colonsay and West Loch Tarbert on the mainland via the Sound of Islay. The introduction of this regular ferry caused arguments with the owners of the ferries from Jura to Knapdale and Craignish, who depended on the Colonsay and Islay traffic.

Sketch by the author of a sailing packet, reproduced from *Summer in the Hebrides*

Sailing packets of various sizes remained on the Colonsay ferry run for most of the nineteenth century. The sketch reproduced by hand from F. Murray's *Summer in the Hebrides* shows one, a 15-ton gaff-rigged sloop. The last island-owned packet came to grief in Scalasaig harbour in the early years of the twentieth century. Another attempt to establish a regular ferry connection between Colonsay, Islay and Oban was made in the 1920s by Duncan Campbell, with his *Isle of Colonsay,* a two-masted sailing vessel with an auxiliary engine. The venture might have succeeded had he been awarded the mail contract.

Apart from these attempts, at the turn of the century, Colonsay's link with Islay and the mainland depended, at least for the transport of passengers, on the MacCallum Orme steamers, calling at approximately ten-day intervals, passengers having to be ferried from the ship to the shore. It seems that the steamers did not keep to a very regular schedule. Mrs Murray wrote in her *Summer in the Hebrides* of 1887: 'Such a boat may advertise to leave Colonsay at 7 p.m. and keep us waiting all night till 7 a.m. without any manner of apology. Many a time we stayed up all night on the "qui vive" [on alert] for the horse whistle which signalled the ferryman to hasten to get all aboard.'

From the 1880s onwards, the MacCallum Orme steamers were the *Dunara Castle* and the *Hebrides,* with the little ex-trawler *Challenger* assisting, although officially she was not to carry more than twelve passengers. Each of these steamers had a turn-round period of about ten days, and it was only when MacBrayne's took over after the Second World War that Colonsay had a passenger vessel call from Islay three times a week.

Postcard showing the *Lochiel* leaving Tarbert on the way to Islay and Colonsay

Since Scalasaig had only a slip and no steamer pier, passengers, cargo, cattle and sheep had to be carried in rowing ferries between ship and shore. These were heavy, clinker-built, wooden boats, about 30 ft in length and 14 ft in beam, propelled by six big sweeps, when there were enough crew to pull them, and manned by a complement of anything from two to twenty. Any willing body was welcome to help. When cattle or sheep were carried on the ferry, a line was sometimes passed on board the steamer, and the ferry was pulled towards the ship. Because the steamer had to anchor outside Scalasaig Harbour, the ferry passage could be quite bumpy, and at one time during the Second World War, the island was cut off for six weeks because the weather did not allow the ferry to meet the steamer.

The first mechanically-propelled ship-to-shore ferry was the *Nestor*, which was fitted with a petrol/paraffin two-cylinder 13.15 h.p. Kelvin engine, of a type known as the 'Poppet Valve'. The engine looked gleaming new but never worked, and a rowing ferry continued to be used. Eventually, the *Nestor* was taken to Oban for her Board of Trade survey, and she disintegrated while being towed back. The next motorised ferry boat appeared after the war around 1949. She was called the *Glassard* and was also driven by a Kelvin 'Poppet Valve' engine. She was damaged while coming alongside a steamer, and when she was being towed to Oban for repairs, someone looked astern to see how she was behaving and saw only the boat's Samson post being towed.

Macbrayne's having replaced MacCallum Orme in 1948, they started to build their own ship-to-shore ferries, first at Barr's of Craigendoran on the Clyde and then at Timbacraft of Faslane, on the Gareloch. They were about

Archie MacPhee, 'The Gordie', ferryman par excellence

35 ft long and 11 ft 6 in to 12 ft in beam, originally varnished, but later painted red, and fitted with J2 Kelvin 22 h.p. diesel engines.

For a time the ship-to-shore ferryman was Sandy McAllister, the uncle of the piermaster's 'Para Mór' ('Big Peter') MacAllister, assisted by Donald 'Gibbie' MacNeill. Donald took over the ferry in 1957.

I have retained vivid memories of the dark winter mornings off Colonsay at that time. The *Lochiel*, having made a very early departure from Port Askaig, would drop anchor off Scalasaig at 8 a.m. Then sheep were 'helped', coaxed and dragged aboard along a plank or two from the ferry boat into the *Lochiel*'s tweendecks.

From 1965 onwards, no ship-to-shore ferries were needed at Colonsay because ships could come alongside the newly-built pier: first the *Lochiel* and the *Arran* from Islay, and then, from 1973, the *Claymore* and the *Columba* from Oban. At the time of writing, the roll-on-roll-off Caledonian MacBrayne vehicular ferries are served by a linkspan at Scalasaig.

For many years, Archie 'The Gordie' and Peter MacPhee of Port Askaig on Islay ran an unscheduled, on-demand, ferry service between Port Askaig and Colonsay. Many stories have been told about The Gordie and his ferry, most of them (including some in Chapter 14) about that 'regular' ferry across the Sound of Islay. However, I have also heard a few about his Colonsay 'sideline'.

One is told about The Gordie ferrying a Lady Strathcona of Colonsay and her lady companion. The ladies were enjoying refreshments en route out of an elegant picnic basket which contained only two cups and saucers. When Lady Strathcona asked, 'Archie, do you mind sharing a cup with me?', he is reputed to have replied, 'I certainly do. I am not in the habit of sharing with other than members of my clan.'

The Gordie was known to be averse to ferrying ministers and policemen. On one occasion, he was asked to fetch a minister from Islay to officiate at a wedding on Colonsay. He reluctantly agreed, on condition that he would put the minister ashore at the point of Colonsay nearest to Islay. While the minister was making his weary way on foot to Scalasaig, the desperate bridegroom phoned Archie's wife, Christine, to ask what had happened to cause the long delay, and she called out the Islay lifeboat!

On another occasion, The Gordie brought some passengers to Colonsay while a couple of Islay policemen were making a routine visit there. They waved to the departing Gordie, hoping he would take them across, but he simply smiled and waved back. When David Clark of the Colonsay Hotel asked him later why he had not picked up the policemen, he said: 'There was no need for police where I was going.'

4

CUAN SOUND AND EASDALE SOUND

Cuan Sound

Cuan Sound, which separates the island of Luing from Seil, is only 200 yards wide. Nevertheless, crossing it in a small boat could be a strenuous affair due to fierce eddies and the tidal stream running through at 6 knots at spring tides. The eddies race along the shores against the flow of the main stream and strike it with force. It has been known for small boats, without the benefit of auxiliary power or with insufficient power, to end up sailing astern through this treacherous and potentially dangerous channel.

The Cuan ferry must have always been the lifeblood of the island of Luing. However, the earliest note of it I have found dates only from September 1888, when John MacIntyre, the Cuan ferryman, used his ferry boat to rescue the district medical officer, Dr Gordon, whose boat, *Gipsy*, capsized between Seil and Luing. John MacIntyre had been the Cuan ferryman for twenty years and was a 'universal favourite' on account of his obliging and genial disposition. In May 1890, a wedding took place at Cuan Ferry on the Luing side. The bride and bridegroom were taken in procession from Cullipool across the island, led by a piper, to be married in the ferry house.

The 1891 *Schedule of Ferries* refers to the Cuan ferry as being worked by one Hector McInnes of Cuan, tenant of Lord Breadalbane, with one large and two small boats. The fares were 2s for a boatload of household furniture, 1s 6d per cart, 6d per horse, 2d per passenger, and children at 1d. In October 1899, a record number of 600 sheep were carried across by the ferry; while sixty cattle were made to swim the Sound. In the same year, Lord Breadalbane had lights fixed at both Cuan ferry landings.

The ferry lost some of its importance to the economic life of Luing with the introduction of steamships. They took on carrying regular supplies for the island and landed them at Blackmill Bay and Toberonochy piers. Between the wars, at least three steamers used to serve the area. Every week, the little SS *Brenda* used to bring wicker hampers of bread and other provisions from Oban to Blackmill Bay. Sheep – in those days selling at 7s 6d or 10s a head – and cattle were shipped from the same pier by the paddlesteamers *Mountaineer* or *Chevalier,* or by the propeller-driven *Princess Louise*. Clyde puffers, making periodic calls at Toberonochy pier, would unload coal and other bulk cargoes. The Cuan Sound ferry was therefore largely restricted to the carriage of passengers. Between the wars, two 15-ft rowing boats served the purpose. One was run from Luing by the two young daughters of a Luing crofter, Nelly and Maggie Nicholson. The other ferry was rowed from Seil by Colin MacFarlane, known as 'Col'. Each boat took five or six passengers, and the standard fare was 3d a head.

Arthur Galbraith of Toberonochy told me of a Blackmill Bay man who, not having any money on him, offered Col a ½d stamp. Col responded by offering to ferry him half-way across the Sound. On another occasion, a couple of men from Luing, which was 'dry' and still is at the time of writing, were returning from having enjoyed a dram at the Tigh-na-Truish Inn on Seil. When they started to argue half-way across the Sound, Col stopped the boat. The men thought they were at Luing pier and stepped overboard.

In the 1920s, a cobble (a flat-bottomed barge) was in use, which needed four or six oars to propel it across. It was intended for the occasional carriage of cattle or sheep. In 1923, it was involved in a somewhat hazardous operation undertaken by Col MacFarlane and Jim Nicholson, the teenage ferrywoman's father, to bring the first motor car to Luing. At high tide, two planks were placed across the ferry's gunwales, the car was carefully driven across the planks and rowed across the narrows. The car in question belonged to Hugh MacCowan of Luing. This undertaking was the precursor of the vehicular ferry, which was not to come on the scene for another thirty years.

After the Second World War, a 25-ft American whaler fitted with a Kelvin 'Ricardo' engine came into service as a passenger ferry. When cattle or sheep were to be ferried, the whaler towed a wooden barge about 20 ft long and 10 ft wide. Such craft were probably built by Macdonald's in Oban.

A new era for the Cuan ferry started in 1953. Argyll County Council introduced the first vehicle-carrying vessel at Cuan, and John MacAllister, a distinguished Second World War commando and formerly a Tarbert fisherman, took on the chief ferryman's job. The new ferry was the *Maid of Luing,* built at Noble's of Fraserburgh. Resembling a fishing boat, she had carvel softwood planking on oak timbers. Being single-ended, she had to be equipped with a vehicle turntable. Her 48 h.p. Gardner engine, driving a single screw, did not provide sufficient power and manoeuvrability for easy operation in the turbulent waters of Cuan Sound, and the ferryman had to charge full ahead or full astern in order to swing her about. The ferry could not cope with full flood or ebb tides, and the Board of Trade decreed that it had to be taken out of service during two hours of flood and two hours of ebb tide. These rules did not take into account the differing conditions at spring and neap tides, with the result that the ferry sometimes operated when it should not have, and sometimes did not operate when it could have done so quite safely. John MacAllister, who remained in charge for nearly twenty years, was famous, among other things, for the large watch by which he ran the ferry and which kept 'Cuan time', usually five minutes ahead of Greenwich Mean Time or British Summer Time.

John MacAllister was still in command in 1972 when the new Cuan vehicular ferry, the *Belnahua*, was built by Campbeltown Shipyard to the order of Argyll County Council. The new vessel, of steel construction, was designed by Mr A. Boyd of Sandbank near Dunoon, the designer of the *Sceptre*, the first post-war Americas Cup Challenger. The launching was a splendid ceremony at which a number of county councillors were entertained. I remember being asked to approach one of the councillors, who happened to be a well-known Argyll minister, to ask him to say grace before lunch. He responded that he should not be expected to do work when off duty.

The *Belnahua*, at 58 ft in length, is 10 ft shorter than originally intended, due to local government economy measures, but being double-ended, her corner ramps can still allow vehicles to drive on and off without reversing and without the use of a turntable. She has twin screws and sufficient power to function at all tides, and she can turn in her own length. The *Belnahua* was still on service in Cuan Sound in the summer of 1991, when I had an opportunity to re-visit John MacAllister on Seil in his retirement, and to listen to his reminiscences. The *Belnahua*'s only deficiency is in her carrying capacity, which is restricted to 12 tons. In consequence, the council bin lorry has to empty Luing's dustbins first, otherwise it would be too heavy for the ferry. In the 1970s, Ian Macdonald, a local man, took over as chief ferryman from John MacAllister, whom he had served as assistant.

The *Belnahua* was registered in Campbeltown at the heartfelt request of Mr Hutchinson, who was the Campbeltown Customs Officer and Registrar of British Ships in 1971. He had a beautiful leather-bound Campbeltown Register of Ships with only one or two names in it. He pleaded for another name to be added, so the owners of *Belnahua* obliged.

Once the *Belnahua* was in service, Roni Cameron of Argyll District Council and I were asked to assess the feasibility and cost of refitting the old *Maid of Luing* for duty as a standby ferry on the Cuan crossing. Our estimate was duly sent to Strathclyde Regional Council, and a few days later, I received a phone call from their office: 'Your estimate is being considered by the committee, but nobody on the committee knows where Cuan is. Can you help?' It was one of those moments when one succumbs to a devilish temptation: 'It is that wee bit of water between the islands of Lewis and Harris,' I said in an as matter-of-fact manner as I could muster. It was not long before the clerk rang again: 'We can't find the islands you mentioned on the map of Strathclyde.' How does one tell members of a regional committee that one has been enjoying a joke at their expense?

Lachy with a real sea dog, Hamish, who went to sea with him every day

The story of ferries to and from Luing would not be complete without a mention of the MacLachlan clan of Cullipool on Luing and Lachlan its late chief, a boat skipper par excellence and a force for good on his island and further afield. The MacLachlans have been tending lights at Fladda, Dubh Sgeir and Eileach an Naoimh, and ferrying people to the islands surrounding Luing including the Garvellachs for several generations. Lachy's ferryman grandfather Lachlan crops up in Miss Donaldson's classic *Wanderings in the Western Highlands* of the 1920s.

In the early 1970s, I surveyed Lachy's ferry which happened to be a converted RNLI lifeboat, and to show trust in my own judgement chartered her to convey a friend's and my own family for a long weekend on Eileach an Naoimh ('Island of the Holy Man'), the southernmost of the Garvellachs, on which St Columba is reputed to have had a holiday abode to escape from the hurly-burly of Iona. I fondly recall his intrepid landing of our party on a precipitous rock face, the boat driven ahead to maintain contact, protected by a thick band of steel up the stem. We were anxious, Lachy impervious to all concern. Once landed, he chugged off, severing our link to safety and security in the hands of this master ferryman, except that before leaving he gave me a distress rocket with which to summon him if a child fell off a cliff. When I repeated the venture twenty years later, I found that Lachy, in association

Landing at Eileach an Naoimh (loaned by the Scottish Ethnological Archive)

with his sons, had expanded the MacLachlan fleet and the MacLachlan clan activities. Unlike many families in the Western Isles, all four generations of that enterprising island family (including Lachy's mother, Lily) were living in Cullipool when I saw them in 1991, all Lachy's children and some grandchildren working at or from Luing, mostly on boats.

In August of 2002 Lachy and his wife Jane went off to sea for three days in their sailing boat. It turned out to be his, like a Viking warrior's, farewell to his ship and to the life at sea which he loved. He died a few days later.

Hubert Duncan, Lachy's friend and partner in at least one of his ferrying enterprises, survived Lachy by only a few months when he died at ninety-five, after nearly forty years on Luing. When Hubert retired from running a garage in Bridge of Weir he moved to Luing and became another of the island's stout men of the sea. He and Lachy were jointly in the business of transporting sheep from Luing to the surrounding islands.

Easdale Sound

Easdale Sound lies some three miles north of Cuan Sound and separates Easdale Island from the west coast of Seil. It is 200 yards wide, but rocks and shoals extending from the shore restrict the navigable channel to 50 ft width in places. It is navigable by small vessels only, and to make its navigation more difficult, the tidal stream can be 1¼ knots strong at spring tides. The island has shrunk in area as a result of slate quarrying, and the channel depth has been reduced by disposal of slate quarrying waste. Some two hundred years ago, Easdale Island was exporting two million slates a year, which figure rose to seven million a hundred years later. This volume of export required a fleet of small cargo ferries running between Easdale pier and the ships anchored in deep water. Even Clyde puffers were sometimes barred from entering the tiny Easdale harbour by a shingle bank.

The earliest record of the Easdale passenger ferry which I have found is a letter of complaint published in the *Oban Times* of January 1893. A correspondent maintained that stopping the ferry service at 8 p.m. endangered life, as it restricted the hours during which a doctor could reach the island, and that other ferries operated till 10 p.m. In 1899, another *Oban Times* correspondent proposed filling in the Easdale channel, and so dispensing with the ferry altogether. Obviously, this suggestion was not put into effect, and in 1900, Lord Breadalbane installed lights at both Easdale ferry landing stages, and the quarrymaster provided a year's supply of paraffin.

By the end of the nineteenth century, there were two kinds of ferries running across the Sound – ship-to-shore and cross-channel – and there were two levels of fares. With MacBrayne's regular steamer, the *Chevalier*, not always able to call at the old wooden pier, a ferry had to carry passengers from her to shore; the charge for this conveyance was 6d. This compared unfavourably with the Ellanbeich on Seil-to-Easdale cross-channel fare of 2d, thus giving rise to visitors' complaints. By 1911, the ferry started to carry Easdale children to and from school on Seil. The ferryman at the time, Duncan McQueen, signed on a second crewman 'in the interests of children's safety'.

Until after the Second World War, the ferry was a private enterprise, the ferryman's wages being paid by the islanders. When the ferryman could not attend to his duties, the islanders had to take it in turn to work the ferry

Easdale (loaned by the Scottish Ethnological Archive)

boat. By the 1940s, the bulk of the island's population of thirty was made up of old age pensioners, who, in the absence of ferryman Peter Duncan's brother, had to do the rowing themselves. Rescue came in the form of one Archibald MacKay. When he heard of the islanders' plight, he gave up his job at Kinlochleven to take up rowing the 16-ft boat across Easdale Sound for the benefit of both passengers and cattle. It was time for Argyll County Council to take the next step.

In 1948, the ferry was taken over by the county council, and in 1949, the small ferry boat was replaced by a stronger 18-ft craft powered by an outboard engine. One of the islanders then said: 'With the new boat and Dugald MacCorquodale running her, we don't feel we are living on an island.'

Dugald was originally a gamekeeper from Scarba, but he became an able and popular ferryman.

A turning point in the history of the Easdale ferry came in 1961. In March of that year, the base of the service was firmly established on the Easdale side of the channel. A new house was provided there for the redoubtable ferryman, Dugald, and it is thought that a horn was also then placed at Ellanbeich pier to call the ferryman from across the Sound. The wooden Dorran prefabricated house was transported to the island in sections by helicopter. In the course of that operation, the roof section of Dugald's new home plummeted into the Sound only yards from the ferry boat. In the end, the construction team fished the roof out of the channel using Dugald's own boat, and within weeks the MacCorquodales were able to move into their new home. It cost the county council all of £2,400.

Setting up the ferry base on the island committed the council to a recurring dredging expenditure to keep Easdale's little harbour clear of slate waste, which is estimated to encroach at the rate of 7 ft per year. Local critics maintained that the wiser course would have been to build on the Seil side, and to lower the sill of the quarry on that side to create a safe harbour there for the ferry boat. While the ferryman was well housed, in effect nothing was done by the council, the providers of the service, to maintain the island's harbour. Apparently, no contractor could be found who was willing to dredge for the money offered by the council, while money must have been spent from time to time on repairs to Easdale pier, although it did not belong to the council, and it could not be reached by the ferry, which had to be moored precariously in the channel.

The controversy over the safety of the ferry landings burst into the open in the autumn of 1961, when Donald Dewar, the local councillor and owner of Ellanbeich pier and most of Easdale island, lost his life while going across. Lord Kilbrandon of Kilbrandon House, Balvicar on Seil, an eminent judge, blamed the council for indirectly causing the fatality by failing to maintain the landings on both sides of the channel. The county council convener retorted that the council, having provided a ferry and a competent ferryman, was reluctant to carry out costly engineering repairs to facilities it did not own for an island population then amounting to fifteen. While the controversy raged, ferry passengers landing on Easdale had to scramble out on to steep and uneven stones. In adverse weather conditions, the island was virtually cut off, and hospital cases would have had to be carried by helicopter.

In September 1978, the 18-ft, outboard-driven open ferry boat was still liable to make landfall on the rocky shore of Easdale Island, although the pier on the Seil side had been improved. On one night that month, the boat got into trouble while crossing in a south-easterly gale. The outboard's shear-pin broke when the propeller struck a rock, so the outboard was out of action, and although the boat had oars, there were no rowlocks, crutches or thole pins, hence rowing was impossible. The ferry was being swept out of Easdale Sound into the open Sound of Insh, but before she cleared Easdale Sound, two of the three on board, a man and a girl, either fell or were swept overboard. The man managed to swim ashore and raise the alarm, as a result of which the girl was found lying exhausted on one of the rocks. It was thought that the third person was still aboard the drifting boat. With the direction of drift being towards Insh Island, the Oban inshore lifeboat was launched to search in that area. The missing man was eventually spotted on an islet off the cast side of Insh Island and picked up by helicopter.

The next crisis occurred in 1989, when Strathclyde Regional Council decided to replace the 18-ft glass fibre boat with an 18-ft flat-bottomed steel barge. The English-built craft was described by the head ferryman, Ian MacFarlane, as 'a skip with an engine in it, fine for an inland loch but useless for Easdale Sound'. Ian and his assistant, Bert Baker, gave the barge a five-week trial before sending it back to the Council's yard at Lochgilphead. The islanders claimed that at 2½–3 knots top speed, the barge was barely capable of coping with the tidal current in the Sound, and christened it 'The Pig'. It was returned once again as the 'standby' boat and has become Easdale's land-based monument to the 'landlubber folly' of the Regional Council. The slowly-growing population of Easdale has since been provided with a Scottish-built, conventional 22-ft long craft as the principal ferry.

In 1992, Bert Baker, who had become head ferryman, retired, and the area engineer in Oban had to look hard once again for someone to take on this, not the easiest of ferrying jobs, before finding the present ferryman.

5
GIGHA

The narrow, flat and green island of Gigha stretches some six miles in the north-south direction parallel to the Kintyre shore and three miles from it. The original ferry landing site, sheltered by Gigalum island, is almost at the southern tip. The township of Ardminish in the bay of that name, the 'capital' of the island, is about one mile to the north.

All could not have been well with the Gigha ferry landing in the middle years of the eighteenth century, because in 1758 the Commissioners of Supply of Argyll 'appointed the five pounds twelve shillings collected on Gigha to be laid out in making the quay at Caolus Gigalus'. Otherwise spelled 'Kelisgiglum', the name refers to the narrows between the tiny island of Gigalum and Gigha, which is the location of the present pier. Two years later, it was recorded that the inhabitants of Gigha were 'appointed to work at Kelisgiglum key and the five pounds twelve shillings allocated in 1758 to be applied.' It seems that this instruction was not fully complied with, because in 1762, 'Malcolm MacNeill brother to Tarbert Surveyor in Gigha parish' was to 'apply eleven shillings and four pence on finishing the quay at Giglum'.

Malcolm MacNeill's report on work in Gigha was approved in 1766, but with the remark that 'the Meeting are ready to doubt the truth of the report, and therefore and because it is surmised that no work has been done on the roads and quays in that island for some time past, the Meeting appoint a Committee for Enquiry into that matter'. Malcolm MacNeill was replaced as surveyor by Roger MacNeill of Taynish. Two years later, the inhabitants of Gigha were to be proceeded against for non-payment of previous years' road and quay money. However, a modicum of progress in completing the Gigha pier must have been made in the following thirty years, because the reference to the 'want of a quay' in the 1792 *Statistical Account* applies only to the Kintyre side of the crossing (to be exact, Tayinloan, then referred to simply as 'Largie', a Macdonald estate extending to that shore).

According to the Commissioners' records of the end of the eighteenth century, the proprietor of the ferry to Gigha was empowered to exact the following freights: 'From one man two shillings, from two or more one shilling each till the number of passengers exceeds five and when that happens they shall pay five shillings amongst them, and no more.' The ferry also features in the records of the Sabbath breaking in the *Gigha Sessions Book* for 1799. In July of that year, two men were accused of ferrying oats from John MacNeill's store at Achamore to Kilberry and to Jura during divine service. The ferryman, Donald MacQuilkan, was exonerated because 'he had been coerced'.

The Revd James Curdie wrote in his *Account of the State of Gigha Parish* in the late 1840s that two ferrymen plied at his time, one from each of the two estates dividing the island, so one was based on Gallochoille and the other on Achnaha, until the Gallochoille Estate was absorbed into the main Gigha Estate in 1865. In Curdie's time, MacBrayne's steamers sometimes met a boat from Gigha, but in 1877, the old *Lochiel* was the first steamer which we know called at Gigha. The Caolas Gigalum pier, which appears to have been abandoned by the ferry some time before 1840, was not rebuilt as a steamer pier until 1895, and before that, steamer passengers had to embark and disembark by a rowing ferry boat. After the amalgamation of the estates, one ferryman had to meet the steamer at whichever 'port' of the island it visited. When the *Lochiel's* successor, the *Glencoe,* came into service on the run with a more complex timetable, the ferryman had to have his wits about him to know where he needed to be with his boat at a given time.

Some time in the 1860s, William Orr, a fisherman of Ardminish, moved into a cottage at Gallochoille known as belonging to the 'Spirit Dealer of Gallochoille' but which became vacant when the island was united. William, probably came in as an assistant, but he took on the job as the steamer ferryman in 1871 and held it until the steamer pier was built. He is reputed to have been quite a character, and his wife, Ellie, was well known for her beauty. In the course of a recent visit to Gigha, I called on Mrs Babs MacNeill, the widow of Angus MacNeill, Willy and Ellie's grandson. She showed me an oil painting dated 1880. In it, Willy's big, wooden shore-to-ship open ferry boat is making its way with huge oars through a very rough sea. The passengers are huddled for comfort and look a bit overwhelmed by the weather.

The Achnaha ferry between the island and Largie on the Kintyre mainland functioned throughout the nineteenth century, towards the end of which it was recorded that there were three ferry boats running, carrying between them 2 tons deadweight. With enviable absence of inflation, their fares were much the same as a hundred years earlier: 2s for a passenger or a bull, 5s for a horse, 6d for a calf, 3d for a sheep and 2d for a lamb. Livestock was thus being moved in spite of the need for 'an improved landing stage at Tayinloan' (Largie) noted in the 1891 *Statistical Account.*

In her *Story of Gigha*, Kathleen Philip quotes a document dated 1885 which confirms the appointment by the island's proprietor at the time, Colonel W.J. Scarlett, of a John Wotherspoon as ferryman. John's remuneration was to consist of the ferry croft, 'except that piece surrounding the house of Mrs MacNeill which she rents'. He could also 'have all the ferry dues'. For this, John had to convey, free of charge, the proprietor and his family, friends and servants, as well as 'such tradesmen and others that may be employed on the proprietor's affairs'. He always had to be ready to do work around the estate, although he was allowed time to work his own croft. When further away than Tayinloan, he had to provide a substitute ferryman at his own expense. In addition to the ferry, he was responsible for 'such boats as Col. Scarlett may happen to have on Gigha at any time, whether for fishing or any other purpose'. John could be dismissed at the laird's pleasure, but he had to give one month's notice. Harsh as the terms of his contract may seem today, John kept on ferrying until the First World War.

Thumbing through the Gigha Register of Births, Marriages and Deaths, I found that between 1805 and 1838, twenty-three people were drowned in the course of being ferried between the 'Largieside' mainland and Gigha in five different incidents, which represents a significant percentage of the population of that time, some 500, lost in relatively infrequent crossings. This leads one to the obvious conclusion that the seas in the Sound of Gigha must be treated with respect. They demand sturdy ferry boats running between adequate piers. This was not always the case, even in the present century.

Until the early 1940s, the ferry boat was a 19-ft long sailing boat called the Broad Arrow, and in the early 1950s, the Achnaha-Tayinloan ferries were still running between the original stone ferry piers, the end of Achnaha pier having by then crumbled away. At times, a dinghy was towed, which allowed the crew to anchor off and row ashore at low water or when heavy surf made coming alongside the pier precarious. At other times, the conditions at Achnaha were such that the ferry had to head half a mile south to the Gallochoille jetty.

Those were the days of Johnnie Macmillan, who skippered the ferry from the 1940s, not infrequently with the assistance of Graham MacCulloch. They had two boats in use in succession to the *Broad Arrow*. The *Village Belle* was a 26-ft, carvel-planked, wooden craft built by Dickie's of Tarbert and powered by a 14 h.p. Kelvin petrol/paraffin engine. The *Jamie Boy* was a 22-ft, Buckie-built clinker-fashion, larch-planked boat with 915 h.p. Kelvin petrol/paraffin E4 engine. She had a slim hull with a sweet, sheer line, as shown in the early photograph supplied by Graham MacCulloch. He also lent me the later photograph, in which her elegance has been spoilt by the erection of a large, square cabin top.

Johnnie Macmillan, known as 'Bimbo', was a tall, well-built native of Gigha. As ferryman for many years, he was highly respected for his boathandling and his knowledge of the waters of the Sound. His asides could be quite penetrating. When hearing of a Tarbert shipwright who fancied

The *Jamie Boy*

himself as a boat designer, he slowly pronounced: 'He is no more a designer of boats than I am a ballet dancer!' The photograph, taken by a lady who used to holiday with the Macmillans, shows Johnnie with Graham MacCulloch in the *Village Belle* at the Achnaha ferry pier. According to Graham, they were taking cattle to the mainland.

It was not until about 1960 that the largesse of the Highlands and Islands Development Board brought about the construction of a landing stage worthy of the name at the Tayinloan ferry terminal. It cost all of £17,000, a considerable outlay in those days. For some time, I had been a little concerned about the *Jamie Boy*, with little power, crossing the three-mile Sound in winter and at night in response to an emergency call. Construction of the sumptuous new jetty provided a good opportunity to appeal to John Smith, the Argyll County Engineer of the day, to fund a ferry boat commensurate with the pier. The outcome was a traditional, 28-ft, wooden, clinker-planked motorboat named *Shuna*. She was built at Crinan Boatyard to a design of Bill Waight, a master boat designer of Cowes, who fetched up at Tarbert in the late 1950s as manager of Dickie's Yard. The acquisition of a sturdier ferry boat called for improvements at the Gigha end of the ferry route.

The Achnaha tidal jetty, conveniently situated in Ardminish Bay, was extended in the 1950s by a steel catwalk which started its life on a tanker. The

The *Jamie Boy* moored at Minister's Pier, Gigha, with the cabin top in place

catwalk extended as far as a rock, onto which passengers could disembark at low water. With a somewhat bigger craft in prospect, there was a need to find a location of a non-tidal landing stage on the Gigha side. Lady Joan Horlick valiantly assisted in the search. She and her husband, Sir James, were deeply involved in the welfare of the island, very much non-absentee lairds. In the end, it was decided to renew the steel catwalk of the Achnaha jetty in wood and to extend it for low-water landing.

The ferryman at the time was Peter Blackstock, a fisherman of Bellochantuy, a township a little way down the coast from Tayinloan. He was ably assisted by his wife, and it was said that the passengers were never certain which one of them was the skipper and which the crew. The Blackstocks' son-in-law, Peter Jamieson, a master mariner normally employed in deep waters, skippered the ferry at times, when home on leave. 'Skipper' Flanders, Peter Blackstock's immediate predecessor, fell victim to a crime of passion which shook the island to its foundations and brought it for once into the national newspaper headlines. His family maintained contact with Gigha for many years after their tragedy.

Peter Blackstock went back to fishing from Bellochantuy in the 1960s, taking the *Jamie Boy* with him, and Ian McKechnie, transplanted from his native Jura to the new ferry house at Ardminish, became the master of first one and then two ferry boats. The *Shuna* was owned by Argyll County Council, and the *Cara Lass* was her near-sister ship, which Ian had built at

Taking cattle to the mainland in the *Village Belle* (loaned by Miss Betty MacNeill)

Crinan on his own account. She was given a little more beam forward to help to lift her bow when loaded. This made her too wide to be taken out through the shed door for launching and the shed had to be partly dismantled. Ian was a reliable, capable and popular ferryman for some twenty years and saw the service through its transition to Caledonian MacBrayne management, when a concrete vehicle ramp was erected alongside the ferry pier. The new steel landing-craft-type vessel of the 'Scottish Islands' class, carrying up to six cars, seemed a far cry from the *Shuna* and *Cara Lass,* but Ian took her and the ramped landing stages in his stride and drove the vehicular ferry until his retirement in the 1980s. Ian and Flora went to live close by the Tayinloan terminal, where Ian's advice could be sought by Graham MacCulloch, who had been Ian's predecessor as a Gigha ferry crew man, and for a time was his successor on the ferry's bridge. Graham MacCulloch was followed in 1991 by Archie Graham and he in 1996 by John Bannatyre. At the time of writing the ferry is being skippered on a roster basis by John Bannatyre, Lachie Wotherspoon, Alasdair McNeill, John Andrew and Freddy Gillies, one time fisherman and editor of the *Campbeltown Courier* and now ferryman and author of several books. The Islands class vessel has been replaced in 1992 by *Lochranza* which carries twelve cars.

In the days of the passenger-only ferry boat, the annual Board of Trade inspections were usually carried out jointly by the ferryman and me on a

The north end ferry being launched (loaned by Miss Betty MacNeill)

slip at Crinan Boatyard, and in time they developed into a bit of a ritual. I would pick up the ferry skipper at Tayinloan jetty an hour earlier than the taxi booked to convey him and his entourage. This allowed an opportunity for us to avail ourselves of a little friendly hospitality en route in a civilised home where it was not considered good manners to water your dram before ten o'clock in the morning.

Until the arrival of the Caledonian MacBrayne car ferry, the service provided by the Gigha ferry was for many years supplemented by MacBrayne's passenger ships on passage from West Loch Tarbert to Islay and Jura. The paddlesteamer *Pioneer* served on that run from 1905; she had a diagonal compound engine, a haystack boiler and unusually small paddles. The *Pioneer* was followed by the motorship *Lochiel,* of 1939 vintage, and later by the Clyde lift-type car ferry *Arran,* converted into a roll-on-roll-off ferry, and by the new car ferry, *Pioneer,* built in the 1970s. They used to call on alternate days at the ships' pier at the southern end of the island. On the days in between, they would, weather permitting, drop anchor off the north end (Port Mór) and be met by a 14-ft rowing ferry – later equipped with an outboard engine – commanded by Gigha's 'Prime Minister' of the day, Angus Wilkinson (later, Seamus MacSporren), who would combine the function of the North End ferryman with those of transport operator, piermaster, storekeeper, postmaster, firemaster and auxiliary constable.

The little ferry carried a varied consignment of passengers and goods, including, on occasion, a Pakistani pedlar with his bicycle and merchandise, and sometimes a calf or a sheep or two. On one occasion, an aunt with her little nephew and niece, whom she was returning to Gigha, spent three days on board the *Lochiel* because on two successive sailings the weather did not allow landing at the north end, and on the intervening sailing a gale prevented the ship from calling at Gigha pier. The photograph shows the north end ferry being launched to go out to the *Lochiel,* with Angus Wilkinson in charge. It is just as well I was not there at the time, because the boat has a perilously low freeboard.

In the early 1970s, Western Ferries, who in those days ran car ferries to Islay in competition with MacBrayne's, attempted regular calls with a vehicular ferry at the north end of Gigha. Sadly, their very exposed linkspan collapsed in the first July gale.

6

IONA AND STAFFA

Iona

Although Iona, a small island off the west coast of Mull, has been a destination for pilgrims from at least the sixth century, when St Columba established his monastery there, there was no ferry landing place on the island for many centuries after that, as far as can be ascertained. There must have been no landing quay on Iona at the time of Boswell and Doctor Johnson's visit in 1773, because they had to be carried ashore by ferrymen. Yet the Maryrs' Bay, a small bay to the south of the present ferry terminal, was the old landing place where bodies of the kings – forty-eight Scottish kings, four Irish kings and eight Norse kings – were brought from Mull. Long after the centre of the kingdom had moved to Scone, kings of Scotland were still ferried to Iona to be buried.

Sir Walter Scott's friend, John Leyden, wrote of the Iona–Oban ferry in his journal in 1800:

> Our boat was only a clumsy open cobble rowed by four unskillful fishermen, with very awkward oars. The most disagreeable circumstance was, that there was no room to lie and hardly any to sit or stand . . . Finally our boat by some mistake had not been sufficiently victualled – as we had now the appearance of continuing all night at sea – we hove to near Carsaig Bay [on Mull] and landed amid a strange cluster of rocks, where we found a hut and procured some goats milk and goats milk cheese but no bread.

In her *Guide to the Beauties of the Hebrides* Sarah Murray tells of having crossed in 1802 from the Ross of Mull to Port-a-Churaid. It was so called because St Columba first landed in his wicker basket at that small bay on the south side of Iona. She landed there on a sloping pebbly beach.

In 1815, Charles Shaw-Lefevre, later Speaker of the House of Commons, described in the diary of his travels how he had to suffer a two-day crossing from Oban to Iona in a 'lime barge, badly built and manned by four of the dirtiest fellows imaginable'. The journey may have tarnished his view of the island, of which he wrote: 'the ruins can boast neither beauty nor grandeur'. Law Lord Henry Thomas Cockburn travelled from Oban to Iona on board the steamship *Brenda* in 1840. He disembarked off Iona into a small ferry boat but could not step ashore without some difficulty.

The following is an extract from one of Dr Mairi MacArthur's books.

As early as 1822, the steamer *Comet* made a trip to Iona and Staffa. The *Highlander* began sailing regularly in 1824. From 1850 onwards, the steamer *Dolphin* called at Iona on every weekday. The tourist route to Iona blossomed after the 1847 Royal Tour. However, it was the need to revive the economy following the 1840s potato famine that brought about the construction of a slip pier in 1850, of about 50 yards length. Prior to that, a natural 'ferry rock', Carraig Fhada ('Long Rock'), in St Roman's Bay was used as a rough landing stage which juts out from the bay below the village. *Lumsden's Steam Boat Companion* used to warn that it could be a damp and dicey landing. In 1837, according to Sir George Head in his *Home Tour of the United Kingdom*, it was sometimes necessary to step across deep chasms, dropping mid-leg deep into hidden pools covered deceitfully by broad slippery sea-weed.

In 1851, Archibald Macdonald, a weaver, was appointed Postmaster of Iona, and a mail reception house was established there. From then until the 1870s, Donald MacInnes collected and delivered mail on foot from Bunessan to Fionnphort on Mull and took it across to Iona by ferry. His wages were 3s per week, and from 1854 the Argyll Estate paid an extra £1 per year for the delivery of the factor's mail. Postal services improved in step with the growth in steam ship traffic. In 1877, a new mail route to Oban via Dalmally speeded up the conveyance of mail to Mull and Iona. The MacBrayne steamer *Pioneer* began to carry a mailbag directly to Iona every weekday of her summer sailings. In winter, the mail service was reduced to three times a week.

The signal for the ferry, reproduced from MacIan's *Highlander at Home*

Crossing the mile-wide Sound of Iona from the Ross of Mull was never a problem for the traveller, because of the number of locally-owned small boats; one simply hired whoever was available for the passage. William Reeves wrote in 1857: 'In calm weather a strong voice may be heard across the straits which are one English mile wide. The only mode, however, now in use for making a signal for a boat is to raise a smoke by burning a bunch of heather. Since each owner of a boat has a particular signal spot, it is at once known on the island whose services are requested.'

Mary Helen McVear, daughter of a Free Church minister for Iona, tells of a group reaching Fionnphort in 1865 to find the ferry boat on the other side. They 'got a smoke set up and rested in Vass's house. John MacCormick's boat came to meet us.'

From the 1850s onwards, a MacGilvray and a MacDougall from the Ross of Mull began to be the usual ferrymen; there are references to allowances for them in the estate accounts, such as: 'for the purchase of a Tiree skiff to serve as a ferry and for carpenter's repairs to her'. The ferry was sometimes used to bring peat across from Mull, as Iona had none. A cart and horse were needed for that enterprise, the cart being taken across on the ferry, while the horses swam.

The Maclean family association with the Fionnphort–Iona ferry was to last for half a century, and for all that time, the crossing was being made by a Tiree-type sailing skiff. Alan Maclean, from Dearghort in the Ross of Mull,

Coll MacLean, 1899 (loaned by the Scottish Ethnological Archive

took on the ferryman's job in 1873, but he died suddenly in 1878, and his young son, Coll, 'Colla Mór' as he was known locally, took over. He was to become a familiar figure on both sides of the Sound of Iona, and in 1929 he received a presentation acknowledging fifty years of unbroken service. During those years, the ferry boat was a double-ended skiff of about 20 ft in length, 8 ft in beam, with a full-length 6 in keel, a single mast forward and a single dipping-lug sail. For the last five or six years of Coll's command, the sailing skiff became a standby to the motorboat he bought. Coll's elder son, Alan, came home from deep-sea service in time to help with running the motorboat engine, which his father rarely touched! This was just as well, as Coll could not have coped with ferrying the growing crowds of summer visitors by sailing boat alone. Alan went back to sea after his father retired, and during the war he served as mate to Captain Colin Macdonald of Iona on the *Ulster Star*. Alan was later master of MacBrayne's *Loch Frisa*. The photograph shows stirks (young cattle) transported on Coll's boat being unloaded at Fionnphort in about 1910. The other photograph, which is also reproduced on the cover, shows Coll's ferry under sail some time before 1928. There is already a motorboat on her mooring, to be seen to the left in the picture.

John Macdonald, an ex-sea captain, started ferrying in 1930 with a 16-ft lug-sail skiff, pending the delivery from MacQueen's of Easdale of his 22-ft

Stirks unloading from Coll's boat. This photograph was taken by a visitor, William Crawford, in the early 1900s (loaned by Dr Mairi MacArthur)

Coll's ferry under sail (loaned by Dr Mairi MacArthur)

Kelvin 'Poppet Valve' motorboat. He carried on until 1943, when Angus MacKechnie, released for the purpose from the Merchant Navy, took the ferry's helm for twenty-two years, assisted by his brother, Dan. Latterly, they were running the *Seagull*, a 32-ft, clinker-built ex-naval harbour launch with a Kitchin rudder.

Alastair Gibson, a local skipper/owner, whose *Glencarradale* was for many years a well-known cargo boat in Argyll waters, ferried from 1 October 1966 to 1973. Apart from the *Seagull*, Alastair used the *Applecross*, a 40-ft ex-American navy launch, originally powered by a Kelvin 44 h.p. engine, later to be replaced by a more powerful Perkins diesel. He acquired her from MacBrayne's, and sold her back to Caledonian MacBrayne when they took over the Iona ferry service in October 1972. Yet another of his ferry boats was the *Jane Gibson*, which preceded the *Applecross* and was not unlike her in size and appearance.

It must have been during the Gibson era that I received a phone call from Lady Gwendoline Lithgow, the very gracious and by then advanced in years matriarch of the Port Glasgow shipbuilding community. She and her friend were apparently in the habit of visiting Iona every year, and on some low water occasions had to follow the narrow, rocky footpath to the ferry landing at Fionnphort. Lady Gwendoline knew of my involvement with the ferries in Argyll and wondered whether I could suggest to her who to talk to to get help for old ladies who had to carry their own baggage up and down the ferry landing. This rather disarming request was, of course, passed on to the right quarters.

When Caledonian MacBrayne took over the Mull–Iona ferry service, together with the *Applecross*, they entrusted it to a Colonsay ferryman, Donald MacNeill, generally known as Donald 'Gibbie'. In addition to the *Applecross*, he had at his disposal the *Craignure* and the *Staffa*. The *Craignure*, another ex-naval harbour launch, carvel-planked, of 35 ft length and 10 ft beam, with a Kelvin diesel engine, used to be the ship-to-shore ferry at Craignure on Mull before a pier was built there. The *Staffa* was a carvel-planked, 32-ft long ex-Largs–Cumbrae ferry powered by a Gardner engine. Early in Donald's era, a pony being carried from Iona to Mull refused to get off the ferry at Fionnphort and in the end kicked Donald's crewman into the water. From May 1979 onwards, Donald operated the service with *Morven*, a 68-ft 'Island' class bow-loading vehicular ferry capable of carrying six cars. She was one of the first two of her class of ferries to be commissioned. Since then the 'Island' class ferry was replaced by a larger 'Loch' class one.

Donald Gibbie was a very safety-conscious skipper. On one occasion, he spotted a young boy sitting on the ferry's bulwark and dangling his feet over the water. Twice he sent his crew to tell the boy in no uncertain terms to come off the bulwark and to stay inboard, but to no avail. On completion of the crossing, the skipper ordered the boy to be brought before him for a thorough telling off. Donald gave the boy a lengthy lecture on the dangers of undisciplined behaviour and on the dire consequences of disobeying captain's orders. Finally, he solemnly asked the boy: 'Do you understand that you will be in real trouble next time you go against the captain's instructions?' The boy politely raised his eyes to Donald and said haltingly: 'I do not understand English.'

The latest of Caledonian MacBrayne's vehicular ferries, the *Loch Buie,* was introduced in 1992. She is 110 ft long, is double-ended and can carry ten cars owned by people on Iona, no other vehicles being allowed on board. The excess deck space is taken up by additional passenger saloons, as nearly all passengers are pedestrians. Her record in 1993, when I was last on board, was 1,300 passengers carried in one day, most of them crossing in the three hours between 11 a.m. and 2 p.m. In accordance with the new regulations which followed the *Herald of Free Enterprise* disaster, she has flashing lights and an alarm which indicate when the ramp door is open.

Quite distinct from the shore-to-shore ferries, the small 'red' ferries have been providing a summer service between Iona and visiting cruise ships at least since the mid-1880s. For about the first thirty years of this century, the passenger cruise ships calling on Iona most weekdays in the summer were MacBrayne's paddlesteamers *Grenadier* and *Fusilier.* They were served by two red-painted rowing boats, about 30 ft long, normally crewed by two Iona men, supplemented by a man from the *Grenadier* who steered. They took forty-five to fifty passengers each. The bow thwart and another just before

The Iona ferry taking passengers from the *King George V*

midships had mast clamps, and two masts and sails were stowed under the thwarts. One 'red' boat used to be towed to Staffa to help the Gometra boat, which was sailed there daily, landing passengers from the paddlesteamer. The 'red' boat could, wind and tide permitting, sail back to Iona under her own power. Otherwise, she had to be rowed all the way back, and the overtime of 2s 6d or 5s was well earned. On rough days only one 'red' boat was manned, with two men on each oar. Sometimes, the boat under *Grenadier*'s stern davits was lowered to assist at Iona, and regularly at Staffa, as the Gometra boat was only a 20 ft skiff.

The *Grenadier* was destroyed in a fire at Oban in September 1927, and the remainder of that season's timetable was fulfilled by the *Fusilier,* running every other day. The *Fusilier* was still coping on her own in 1928, and in order to save time, Captain Maclean of Iona was hired to tow the 'red' boats with his motorboat – the first use of the motorboat in shore-to-ship ferrying. From 1929, John MacInnes of Iona handled both Iona and Staffa landings with his two motorboats. In the early 1930s, the *Loch Fyne,* a brand-new MacBrayne motorship, the first diesel-electric vessel, took up the service and distinguished herself at once by treating passengers to continuous vibration. About the same time, MacBrayne's themselves provided two motor ferries, the *Staffa* and the *Iona,* to be run by John MacInnes and his local crews. George Bergius, a retired director of the well-known engineering company of that

The *Ulva, Lochshiel* and *Iona* (loaned by the Scottish Ethnological Archive)

name, which made Kelvin engines, knew John MacInnes well and recollects that when John visited the Kelvin office in Glasgow's Dobbie's Loan, his voice could be heard all over the place. From 1936 until the war, in which she played a distinguished part, the *King George V* served on the Iona summer run. The vessel, built in 1926 for Williamson Buchanan, had the elegant appearance of a miniature two-funnel liner, and boasted the first geared turbine propulsion and had originally been fitted with high-pressure boilers.

After the war, the *Loch Fyne* came to Iona on alternate days until the *King George V* resumed service in 1947. She was employed on the Iona run for ten summer weeks a year. During that time, six days a week (later, only four), she would circumnavigate the island of Mull, taking the north or south route to Iona and Staffa on alternate days. At Iona, a ferry boat would pick up passengers through the 'ferry door' on the lower deck. Many families, including my own, have fond memories of the agility and kindness with which the Iona ferry crews handled very old and very young passengers as they emerged through *King George V*'s 'ferry door'.

Having completed her summer stint, the *King George V* enjoyed the leisured comfort of Greenock's East India Dock for the remainder of the year. This 'comfort' extended to an all-year-round 'speed allowance' for the captain and chief engineer by virtue of their ship being the only one in the MacBrayne fleet capable of speeds in excess of 18 knots. The special character of the *King George V* was matched in the 1960s by the personalities of her mate and chief engineer. The mate was 'Big John' MacCallum, a native of Tiree and a master

Landing on Iona in 1922 (loaned by the Scottish Ethnological Archive)

at repartee. He would stand at the top of the ship's gangway and, out of the corner of his mouth, pass remarks about those coming and going. When a well-known church dignitary appeared carrying a pastoral staff, John was heard to mutter: 'Look at this – one crook supporting another.'

Prior to the ship's spring departure for her Iona service, I would be busy with her annual survey. Sometimes, the hinged shutters to the bulwark's freeing ports were found to be rusted up solid, so preventing the clearance of water from the decks. 'Big John' would plead: 'You chust leave them alone, Meester Surveyor, they will work themselves loose by and by.' Archie MacVicar, the chief engineer, hailed from Ardrishaig. He was of a kind and romantic disposition, but was inclined to dwell on little worries. Big John was always ready to console him with appropriate advice. When Archie thought he might be running out of boiler oil, Big John would soothingly whisper: 'It's all right Archie, there will be plenty of peat on Mull.' The last evening of *King George V*'s Iona season was known in Oban as the 'MacVicar Follies'.

The *King George V*'s shore-to-ship Iona ferries were the 35-ft *Ulva* and *Iona*, purpose-built at Timbacraft of Faslane, on the Gareloch. They were still of wooden construction, but beamier than the previous ferry boats, and now fitted with Kelvin diesel engines. The first ferryman-in-chief was Captain Neil MacInnes, followed by Willie Macdonald, and from 1955, Archie Macdonald. He was assisted by Jonathan Dougal, whose son, Ian, breeds sheep and Highland cattle on Iona (several other locals were involved over the years).

Archie MacArthur's *Sgoth Mhor* taking laundry baskets and wool sacks out to the *Dunara Castle*, in the 1920s (loaned by Dr Mairi MacArthur)

When the *King George V* was retired from the Iona service in September 1974, the same ship-to-shore ferries attended the motorship *Columba*, which maintained the summer cruises to Iona until 1988. However, the 'wee' ferries were abandoned with the arrival of the first passenger/vehicle shore-to-shore ferry, *Morven*, in 1979. She was adapted for occasional use as a tender to the cruise ships by having a gangway door cut in her bulwark and by the provision of inflatable fenders.

Apart from the weekly summer visits to Iona by a cruise steamer, a regular all-year-round passenger/cargo service from Glasgow to Iona was maintained by the M. Orme and J. MacCallum shipping companies from the last quarter of the nineteenth century. The companies amalgamated to form the MacCallum Orme Shipping Company in 1929. Their cargo/passenger vessels, the *Dunara Castle* and the *Hebrides,* had ten-day turnaround services on different, complementary routes, and were later assisted by the smaller *Challenger,* a trawler converted to a cargo carrier. The shore-to-ship ferries attending the MacCallum Orme ships were for two generations in the able hands of the MacArthur family. Prior to 1931, the 20-ft ferry owned and rowed by Archie MacArthur was the *Sgoth Mhor* ('Big Skiff'). In 1931, the *Anna Sona* was acquired by the MacArthurs as the first powerboat on the MacCallum Orme ferry run. She was about 25 ft in length, clinker-built and with a Kelvin 'Ricardo' engine which superseded the original Kelvin 'Poppet Valve' engine. When required, the MacArthur ferry boat towed a wooden cargo barge about 30 ft in length. The barge often carried sheep and cattle, accompanied by their drovers, to be transferred into the steamer's tweendecks and landed – ahead of any passengers – at Merkland Quay in Glasgow.

In 1948, the MacCallum Orme cargo/passenger service was taken over by MacBrayne's, who introduced their own cargo ships, the *Loch Broom, Loch Carron* and *Loch Ard*, on the Western Isles circuit, which included Iona. This required a cargo ferry, for which Neil MacArthur continued to use his own motorboat at first, and later a MacBrayne boat, the *Soay*. The *Applecross* was in service from 1965 while she alternated between MacBrayne and Gibson ownership. The ship-to-shore cargo ferrying lasted until the early 1970s, when the MacBrayne cargo ships were phased out and the *Applecross,* now finally under Caledonian MacBrayne's ownership, became the shore-to-shore cargo ferry. This cargo ferrying, along with all the other small boat ferrying in the Sound of Iona, came to an end in 1979 with the arrival of the *Morven*. The new 'Island' class ferry could carry either six Iona-owned cars or a smaller number of Iona-bound goods-supplying vehicles.

Staffa

Some 200 years ago, Staffa, a tiny island about five miles north of Iona, was already a starred item in the Western Isles tourist itinerary, its attractions including the famous Fingal's Cave, but being ferried there could be an adventure. John Stoddart, who arrived in Oban in 1799, found that the accepted price of a round trip to Staffa was 15s and two bottles of whisky. He pointed out for the benefit of those who might come after him that it was by no means unusual to have to wait a fortnight for fair weather, and even if you did set sail, it did not mean that your boatmen had any intention of landing you on Staffa:

> Our excursion afforded us a proof of that respectful deference with which people here, probably for interested motives, consult the inclinations of their wealthy passengers. In the narrow Sound of Ulva [between Mull and the Isle of Ulva] the sea was heaved into huge, white breaking surges by most violent gale and we were driven along so rapidly that had we struck on any of the bold pointed rocks, by which we were surrounded, we must have been instantly dashed to pieces. After a little experience of this dangerous navigation, finding that the more we advanced into the open the more tremendous it appeared, I asked the only one of our boatmen who understood English, whether we could possibly get to Staffa. He answered 'assuredly not'. Pressed to know why they have taken us on so fruitless an errand he replied that 'it was merely in compliance with your wish to set sail'.

The *Inverness Courier* reported from Staffa on 22 July 1835: 'The boatmen had been brought from Iona and they instantly set themselves to light some lanterns and form torches of old ropes and tar with which they completely illuminated the ocean-hall into which we were ushered . . . The boatmen sang a Gaelic jorram or boat song in the cave, striking their oars violently in time with the music.'

At the time of writing, there are at least three robust Staffa ferries which ply from the Sound of Iona, and provided the weather is not too severe, one can make the crossing to Staffa in something like forty-five minutes. The route to Staffa from Lagganulva on Mull can be even quicker.

7

JURA TO KNAPDALE AND CRAIGNISH

From early times raising Highland black cattle to be exported live to the southern markets was the major source of income in Scotland, and this trade increased in importance after the Act of Union with England in 1707, and especially after clan warfare ceased. Jura, being close to the Knapdale mainland, was the obvious 'land bridge' to convey cattle from Islay and Colonsay to market. According to Thomas Pennant, Jura received 1,700

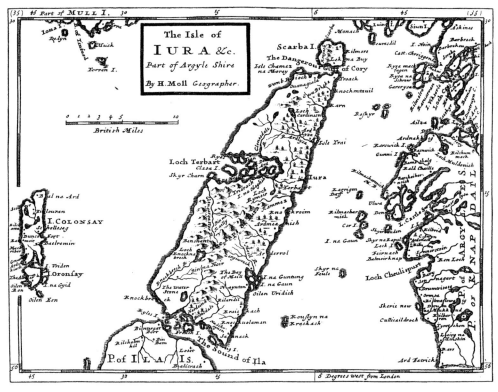

1725 map of Jura by Herman Moll (largely based on Blaeu's map of 1654) (loaned by Norman Tait)

Islay and 300 Colonsay cattle in 1772. Between 1,000 and 2,000 cattle were exported from Jura every year in the early part of the nineteenth century.

At that time, cattle from Islay, having been ferried across the Sound of Islay to Feolin, were driven through Jura, keeping to the eastern side of the island, northwards to Loch a' Bhaille Mhargaidh (or 'Market Loch', as it is also known). Here, cattle from Islay were joined by Jura cattle gathered at the lochside. From there, the combined force of drovers made their way north-eastwards, to arrive at Lagg on the evening of the next day, the drove route keeping them well away from the crofts. At Lagg, likely as not, the same gabbarts which had ferried them across the Sound of Islay were waiting to carry them across the Sound of Jura to Keills on the Knapdale mainland.

Cattle from Colonsay or Oronsay were ferried to Ruantallain on Jura, on the north side of the mouth of Loch Tarbert. They were driven along the north shore of the loch and up the east shore of the island to Kinuachdrach, at the north-eastern tip of the island. Some Colonsay cattle were landed at Corpach Bay on the north-western shore of Jura and driven along Cruaidh Ghleann and Glen Grundale to the east shore at Ardlussa, and then north to the Kinuachdrach rock jetty, to be ferried to Aird on the Craignish peninsula. These crossings were hazardous due to the tides and eddies of the Gulf of Corryvreckan, off the north shore of Jura, and the perilous waters of Dorus Mór off the mainland, where the tide sweeps round Craignish Point.

Disputes over the right of way for Colonsay cattle brought about litigation between the MacNeills of Colonsay and the Campbells of Jura. Eventually, a settlement was reached between James Campbell, proprietor of the Tarbert lands of Jura, and Alex MacNeill of Colonsay, the proprietor of the Jura lands of Ardlussa and Barnhill. The settlement agreed the passage of Colonsay droves across Jura, from Ruantallain on the north side of the mouth of Loch Tarbert to Ardlussa, Knockintavil (Barnhill) and Kinuachdrach on the east shore.

Another dispute arose in the early part of the nineteenth century between the Campbells of Shawfield, who were the owners of Islay, and the Campbells of Jura about the Islay cattle, now so heavy as to be unable to use the route over the hills, stamping along the lightly-constructed new road from Feolin to Lagg. Not only was the road built at that time, but also the stone piers, slipways and cattle enclosures at Feolin and Lagg. They still stand almost as good as new and are a tribute to the skill of not only the famous civil engineer, Thomas Telford, but also the local designer, David Wilson, and the local engineer James Hollinsworth.

The story of the Jura ferry piers before Thomas Telford's time which emerges from the mid-eighteenth century records of the Commission of Supply for Argyll is the usual one of promises and delays. Generally speaking, Jura people north of Ardlussa and those from the Isle of Scarba were expected to work for three days in the summer on the quay at Kinuachdrach, and Jura people south of Ardlussa were to look after the Feolin and Lagg piers. The people of Craignish parish were to concentrate on the quay at Aird, and the inhabitants of Provost James Duncanson's lands were held responsible for the quay at Keills, west of Loch Sween in Knapdale. It appears that the maintenance work commissioned in the 1740s and '50s must have been substandard, because in 1761, Glendaruel was appointed to check the report from Jura and to oversee the work at Kinuachdrach. A year later, some unauthorised use of statute labour had to be stopped. Referring to the landing at Ardfin, at the south end of Jura, it was decreed that it was not 'a publick ferrying place and any further work at the harbour thereof is discharged'.

In the same year, James Duncanson of Keills applied for £10 to repair the quay at Kilvickocharmaig, in the parish of North Knapdale. This was granted, provided that he kept the pier in constant repair thereafter. Two years later, the same proprietor came back for another £15 towards erecting a quay at the same ferry place. In response, a committee was appointed, consisting of Stonefield, Dunnardy and Dunna, to consider the application in light of the proposal to remove the ferry from Keills to Barnashally on the Knapdale side and from Lagg to Ardlussa on the Jura side. The committee's report of 1765 proposed 'commuting the labour of four hundred people to moneys' for extending the road from Lagg to Ardlussa. The new scheme must have been viewed with an element of doubt, because in the mean time, the proprietors of Keills and Lagg were appointed to keep good boats and accommodation for ferrying passengers and cattle. The northern ferry between Kinuachdrach and Aird did not seem to be affected because, in the same year, the inhabitants of Craignish parish were to work on the road from Gartcharran to the ferry at Aird.

A permanent ferry boat was stationed at Aird well into the nineteenth century. It was recorded in 1843 that the parish of Craignish possessed a small vessel chiefly employed for ferrying to and from Jura. However, this was never the principal crossing from Jura – out of the 4,000 or so sheep and black cattle said to have been ferried that year, the majority crossed from Lagg to Keills.

The drovers who accompanied the cattle to the markets just under a hundred years ago were paid at the rate of 1s per day plus their food. They were expected to make the return journey at their own expense. Jura's last link with the cattle traffic of those days was broken with the death some years ago of John MacLean of Lagg. He spent all his life on Jura as a cattleman, shepherd, and later as stalker on the Tarbert Estate. He could remember crossing, as a boy, from Lagg to Knapdale with the drovers and receiving 2s 6d for his services. He had to return on his own, and this he did with some anxiety, as there was no regular ferry service once all the cattle had been ferried. He died in his eighties.

On the Knapdale side of the Lagg ferry, there are the remains of a cattle landing slip in Carsaig Bay, and the stone landing pier at Keills still stands intact in a little bay facing south-west. I have spoken to men who remembered cattle droves from Jura passing over that pier in their youth. I was told that due to the shallowness of water surrounding the pier, the open ferry boat was of shallow draft. The boats were wide in the beam, single-masted, with heavy oars to help in calm weather. To lighten the load as the ferries approached the harbours, beasts were often thrown overboard in deep water to swim ashore.

A hundred years earlier, James Hogg told in his *Highland Tours* of seeing two cows swimming – one exhausted with her side uppermost – in the sound of Jura:

> We were lost in conjecture where these cows could have come from, there being no other vessel within sight from which they could have made their escape. I could think nothing more probable that they were beasts which have been lately ferried from Jura and were attempting to swim the Sound to their native isle, a distance, I suppose, not exceeding eight miles, but you know as much as I do.

The ferry inn at Lagg has been a farmhouse for many years, and Thomas Telford's ferry pier and slipway have not seen much traffic for a long time. Joseph Mitchell, one of Telford's engineers, writing in 1883 in his *Reminiscences of My Life in the Highlands,* described his experience of the Lagg Inn and ferry as follows:

Lagg pier (loaned by Dr Arthur Kitchin)

On arriving at the ferry we found every corner of the Inn crowded with drovers who had been detained by the weather for several days and were passing their time, as is their wont, in riotous and continuous drinking. We felt it no agreeable sojourn to stay at the Inn with these half-intoxicated men, for the very air was impregnated with an odour of whisky. We appealed to the ferrymen to take us across. At first they positively refused on account of the storm, but with some persuasion and a handsome present, their scruples were overcome and they prepared for the voyage. No sooner had the drovers heard that the boat was to cross at our request than they got excessively angry, talked in Gaelic long and loud, and insisted that we should take at the same time a cargo of their cattle. This the boatmen could not refuse and eighteen cattle were put on board.

The boat was of a great width of beam and the cattle were fastened with their heads tied to rings on the gunwale on either side. We had also the chief drover's pony which stood in the middle of the boat. The wind was quite in our favour, but it blew furiously and the sea was high. At last we cleared the land and got into the channel. How the wind did roar and how the cattle struggled to get their heads free. The extent of sail we carried was forcing the bow too deep into the sea and there was fear of being swamped. The men tried to lower the sail which in their agitation they could not effect.

On this, the chief drover seized the helm and with sharp and decisive words took command of the boat. By his admirable steering he relieved her a good deal. We had to take the narrow and rocky entrance, a most difficult navigation, but the drover's sharp and distinct orders were promptly obeyed and in no time he landed us in shelter within a little bay. The time we took to make the crossing – nine miles – was little more than half an hour. I shall never forget the Lagg ferry or the gallant Highland drover who, by his prompt and decided action, was the means under Providence of saving our lives.

While there has been no regular ferry between Jura and the mainland for many years now, Donald Darroch, for a long time gamekeeper at Inver and farmer on the north-east shore of Jura, remembered mail being carried from Crinan directly to Kinuachdrach, which was, and still is, very difficult to get to by road. Until the Second World War, mail went by pony and trap from Craighouse only as far as Ardlussa. The part-time ferrymen were the MacKinnons, who lived in a small house at Kinuachdrach. Charlie MacLean of Craighouse on Jura told of these ferrymen enjoying their visit to the Crinan Hotel so much on some occasions that they would come back to Jura without the mail!

I have also been told that one of the MacKinnons who worked the crossing from Crinan to Kinuachdrach could judge the wind and tide so reliably that he could sleep on the bottom of the boat while she was drifting across. He was in the habit of buying a bottle of whisky when he was at Crinan; half of it would be consumed before he got into the boat, and then he would set off alone. One day, he was accosted by a new minister, who suggested that it was unwise for him to be by himself in the boat, to which his reply was: 'And who said I was alone?'

In the 1950s, the Fletchers of Ardlussa allowed Ian McKechnie, skipper of their 36-ft motor launch, *Lady Ailsa,* to ferry people to and from Carsaig. Apart from carrying the summer holidaymakers, the ferry sometimes had to act as a seaborne ambulance and respond to all kinds of emergencies. One New Year's night, Ian had to come straight from a dance to convey a woman in labour across the Sound of Jura. Another time, a man in a state of mental breakdown was brought to him by the Jura doctor, who promptly left his patient in Ian's care to be ferried to Carsaig single-handed and without any medical assistance. On yet another occasion in the 1950s, Ian, along with Alaistair Shaw, had to use the ferry as a salvage tug to save the Glasgow puffer *Raylight* from coming to grief in Corryvreckan Whirlpool. The *Lady Ailsa* was also used to tow a cobble full of slates across the Sound.

In 1958, the Ardlussa 'ferry' was augmented by the acquisition of a smaller motorboat – the *Caughoo.* Later in the 1960s and early '70s, after Ian departed Jura to take over the Gigha ferry, a 30-ft ex-naval pinnace, the *Fiona*, became the Ardlussa ferry boat, with a boatman by the name of Brian, who has had some inconclusive dealings with the Board of Trade Marine Survey Service, in the person of the author. On the occasion of the Craighouse Regatta, some friends and I hired this ferry to bring a party of friends from Carsaig. Just as the two parties were impatiently straining their eyes through binoculars to spot each other on opposite sides of the Sound, Brian sent a message that he couldn't make the crossing, as the Board of Trade surveyor would not approve of his ferrying in rough weather. He was later discovered sheltering from the force three to four easterlies in a snug corner of the Craighouse Hotel bar.

Mike Richardson, who had come to live with his wife and family at Kinnachdrach, was in the 1980s running a kind of outward-bound centre and guest house there. In connection with this he had been providing a ferry service to Crinan as required. At one time he had the contract to collect at Crinan Sunday papers for Jura and Islay.

John Green of Perth tells of crossing in the summer of 1987, with his bicycle, on Mike Richardson's scheduled Sundays-only run from Kinuachdrach to Crinan. The crossing started before 6 a.m. in order to collect Sunday papers for Jura and Islay. Apparently the cost for an individual crossing would have been £25 plus £1 for the bicycle, but that was modified when undertaken on the early Sunday morning run and when combined with the cost of a night in Mike's fairly basic 'bunkhouse' and breakfast.

For many years now, the Lagg–Keills crossing has been advocated as the first leg of the so-called 'overland route' to Islay demanded by some Islay residents. The main difficulty would be the lack of an all-weather anchorage suitable for a large vehicular ferry on either side of the Sound of Jura.

8

KERRERA

The Island of Kerrera, barely five miles long, lies in the Firth of Lorn, between Oban and Mull, close to the Lorn mainland. It forms a natural 'stepping stone' to Mull and the islands beyond, but to serve that purpose, the island needed a ferry on either side: a 'small' one across the barely ½-mile-wide narrows between what is now known as Port Kerrera on the eastern shore of the island and Gallanach on the Lorn shore, and a 'great' ferry between the western shore of Kerrera and a landing near Auchnacraig on Mull, at the mouth of Loch Don, now known as Grass Point, a crossing of some three miles. This ferry system was always a precarious one, because the waters between Mull and Kerrera are among the wildest on the west coast, and because Kerrera does not have an all-weather anchorage. Making a landfall on the west or south coast of Kerrera can be risky when a strong wind from west-south-west to south meets a flood tide or when a strong south-easterly meets an ebb tide.

The ownership of the ferries has been in the hands of the MacDougalls, the lairds of Dunolly, for a very long time. To quote from early family documents, the 'ferry has been exclusively possessed by Dunolly and his predecessors beyond all memory of man'. In 1622, a complaint was lodged against the 17th laird of Dunolly, Sir John MacDougall, for levying a toll on cattle ferried from Mull to Lorn. Later in the seventeenth century, the Ardmore lands in the south of Kerrera, from which the Mull ferry used to run, and the ferry rights were forfeited by the 19th laird of Dunolly and only redeemed by the 23rd laird.

In the first half of the eighteenth century, the Mull ferries used to run from Ardmore in the south and Slaterach in the north, but by mid-century, the ferry port was moved to Barr-nam-Boc ('Barnabuck') Bay on the west side of Kerrera, which was more central and more sheltered from the southwesterlies than Ardmore. As early as 1749, the inhabitants of Kerrera were required to perform three days' work on the Barnabuck ferry quay every year.

In 1756, the Auchnacraig-Kerrera ferry freight charges were laid down as 8s Scots for each black cow between 1 January and 1 July and 10s Scots from 1 July to 1 January.

In 1759, Sir Donald Campbell of Airds, known as 'Black Sir Donald' or 'Domhnull Dhu Nan Airds', then factor to the duke of Argyll in Mull, complained on his own behalf and that of Angus Grigorson, tacksman of Auchnacraig and the Auchnacraig ferry, that Lieutenant Dalton, with a party of soldiers, had press-ganged two young men employed on the ferry, carried them to Leith and put them on board Captain Ferguson's ship. 'The inhabitants are now in such terror of being pressed that it is almost impossible to find men to work on the ferry. A great number of cattle require to be ferried.'

In 1760, Alexander, the 23rd laird of Dunolly, applied to the Commissioners of Supply for Argyll for financial assistance of £14 towards blasting rocks at Barnabuck, thus making a safer mooring for the ferry boat. He argued that placing the ferry landing half-way between the alternative ports of Ardmore and Slaterach would benefit the 'liadges' (feudal tenants) and make for a safer crossing. The quay at Barnabuck was already under construction two years earlier, or so it would appear from workmen's receipts dated 1758: 'Received by Hector Maclean blaster and quarrier the sum of three pounds and fifteen shillings as payment for ninety days' work performed at the pier of Barnabuck at ten pence per day', and 'Received by Donald Sinclair smith the sum of two pounds and five shillings for ninety days' work at sixpence per day'. There is also a material account which includes '3 stone and 11 ounces of iron at sixpence per pound'. Communication must have been precarious at the time, because in May 1760, the Commissioners complained that MacDougall had given no report on his doing anything to the quay at Barnabuck.

The ferry route between Auchnacraig and Barnabuck and on to the mainland by the 'small' ferry remained in service for another century, but it was not all smooth sailing. Dunolly kept complaining that he would not be able to maintain the ferry boats if his service was bypassed by a direct one from Mull to Oban. The 1793 opinion of the justices of the peace and Commissioners of Supply was that the bypass ferry was a matter of 'progressive improvement', but that the ferries to Mull via Barnabuck could not be dispensed with. The controversy was eased by accepting the recommendation that the fare for saddled horses be raised to 2s 6d.

Sarah Murray, in her *Companion and Useful Guide to the Beauties of Scotland,* describes the delights of the Auchnacraig ferry at the turn of the eighteenth century. The ferry put to sea full of Mull cattle southbound. The two sailors, who spoke little English, were bustling with the sails in a high wind. Sarah asked if the boat was in danger of going to the bottom. 'Oh yes,' was the answer repeatedly given by both men, but 'she perceived their countenances did not accord with significance of those words'. As soon as the sails were hoisted and the boat was in proper trim, the boatmen started to examine the parcels she seemed to take the most care of. One took a little mahogany box and, balancing it in his hand, enquired, 'Is monies?' Sarah opened the box and presented each of them with a small tumbler of wine out of it. Some of her English friends later commended her presence of mind on this occasion.

In 1817, sheep were introduced to Mull, and this exacerbated the problem. Sheep, unlike cattle, could not swim across the narrows, and the tendency was for the Auchnacraig ferrymen to take them directly to Dunolly Farm on the mainland, where they trampled the crops. This added insult to injury inflicted on the Kerrera ferry receipts.

The seasonal droving of cattle was a large-scale movement. In the early part of the nineteenth century, as many as 2,000 cattle from Coll, Tiree, Mull and even Morvern would gather on Kerrera in the fanks (sheep folds) at Ardmore. They would then be driven to the north end of the island and swum across the narrows at Rhu Cruidh ('Cow Point'), which is on a tidal island, and which provides the shortest crossing. The bay and the land immediately to the south of that point are known as Ardantrive (Ard-an-t'snàimh, 'Point of Swimming'). The laird of Ardantrive was naturally concerned about his crops. Dunolly offered to introduce a big 22-ft ferry boat with a crew of four men to put an end to cattle swimming between Ardantrive and Dunolly. The boat was built at Port Kerrera, where a boatbuilding yard was established in the first half of the nineteenth century. A record of 1853 refers to two large trees being supplied for two oars, and two for another large ferry at Port Kerrera. At that time, a 22-ft ferry boat was valued at £24, its keel costing 12s.

The large ferry boats for carrying cattle droves were beamy and well-tarred inside and out. The bilges were protected with brushwood bedding, and the inside of the gunwales had rings for securing cattle during the passage. The nominal capacity of such a ferry boat was four cows, eight stirks or fifty sheep, but these numbers were often exceeded.

Fares for passengers and beasts remained unchanged from the mid-eighteenth century until 1813, when an increase was allowed to 1s 6d for a foot passenger, but only 6d when that passenger was attending fewer than twenty-one sheep. (Presumably the foot passenger paid nothing if he had more than twenty-one sheep.) Sheep were to be charged at 2s 6d for a lot of ten. The Kerrera residents could pay their dues in kind on an annual basis. In the 1840s, the average 'ferrymoney' paid by a Kerrera tenant to Duncan MacDougall, the ferryman, was three stooks of corn and two pecks of meal.

By 1850, there were more complaints about drovers bypassing the Kerrera ferry, this time directed at the Auchnacraig ferryman on Mull. He replied that 'dealers will go where they please and often by boats other than the ferry boats'. At one stage, a compromise petition was made to the Commissioners suggesting regulations which would permit passengers to be ferried directly between Mull and the mainland, but would require cattle to be ferried via

Kerrera. The Kerrera ferryman would be entitled to remuneration should any beasts need to be ferried directly. The compromise arrangement did not survive for very long. The age of steam had come, and as early as 1823, Lord Breadalbane foresaw that steam propulsion would soon allow cattle boats to be towed from Mull to the mainland. Another incentive to transport the Mull cattle directly to Oban was the creation of a cattle market there, and so, half-way through the nineteenth century, the 'long ferry' fell into disuse for carrying passengers and cattle.

The Royal Mail continued to be ferried from Mull via Kerrera for a little longer, as it had been continuously for a hundred years. From the beginning of the postal service in the mid-eighteenth century, all mail from Mull, Iona, Coll and Tiree came to the mainland via Kerrera. As late as 1856, the postmaster general considered steamboats to be too unreliable to carry mail. The GPO in Scotland made regular, annual contributions to the 'long' and 'short' Kerrera ferries: in 1823, £36 was paid towards the former, and £5 towards the latter. The Oban postmistress distributed the money between the ferrymen at the three points of departure: Barnabuck, Auchnacraig and Port Kerrera. Ferrymen were also sometimes given financial assistance to purchase new sails. However, in 1865, the 'long' ferrymen justified their claim to a bigger subsidy not only by the loss of passengers to the steamships, but also by the fact that two boats had to be kept both at Auchnacraig and Barnabuck: a rowing boat for calm weather and a sailing one for when there was wind, with at least two men for each boat.

By the 1860s, Mull people started pressing for a six-day postal service directly to and from Oban. In response, a special sailing smack was built to enable the Auchnacraig ferrymen to make the direct passage. The sailing smack was not replaced by a steamboat until the 1880s. The advent of the regular, direct link was the last straw for MacDougall of Dunolly, the proprietor of the 'long' ferry, and for Angus Mackinnon, the ferry's skipper, and they petitioned for its discontinuation; and so the ferry between Auchnacraig and Barnabuck came to an end in 1864. The pier at Barnabuck, although out of use since then and crumbled somewhat by weather and age, is still plainly recognisable.

To this day, mail from Kerrera is still carried by the Port Kerrera ferryman, and when a sub-post office was established on the island in 1879, the ferryman's wife became the postmistress at Port Kerrera. The recent ferryman's house is the old Port Kerrera Inn. It was one of the three ferry changehouses (inns or alehouses) on the island. The one at Ardmore was older than the one at Barnabuck, but the one at Portninachar (the original name for Port Kerrera) had been in use the longest. According to travellers at the turn of the eighteenth century, the latter was reckoned to have 'accommodation of the most limited description'. The Auchnacraig changehouse was at that time

The old Port Kerrera Inn (loaned by Dr Arthur Kitchin)

considered to be better for people, but not for horses. There, the ostleress thought that 'it was not proper to give food of Christians to horses'. The importance of a reasonable standard of accommodation at the inns in those days can be judged from the fact that passengers sometimes had to spend a couple of nights at the Auchnacraig ferry changehouse waiting for the weather to moderate.

In spite of the importance of Kerrera as a ferry 'stepping stone' between the Inner Hebrides and the mainland until the mid-nineteenth century, relatively little effort appears to have been put into the building of ferry slips and drove roads on the island until well into that century. Although the quay at Barnabuck was made suitable for unloading cattle at all states of the tide in about 1760, the Port Kerrera slip was not extended for loading at low-water spring tides until about 1830. It was only in 1801 that a commission was set up under Patrick MacDougall of Dunolly to plan a drove road across the island between Port Kerrera and Barnabuck, along with enclosures intended to prevent cattle from straying and damaging crops. The road between the two ferries, which was opened in 1832, has both southern and northern arms. The reason behind the two drove routes becomes apparent to anyone who has completed the whole circuit on foot: a choice was being provided between the easier and the shorter route. The southern route is flatter but longer, and the northern one steeper but shorter. Owing to the absence of motor car traffic on the island, both routes are in the same condition today as when they were built to the early nineteenth-century drove road standard.

Before the drove roads were made, crossing Kerrera on foot from ferry to ferry must have entailed a steep and long walk. So it would appear from Boswell's account of how Lochbuie persuaded the Auchnacraig ferryman to make a direct passage to Dunolly in order to save Doctor Johnson 'the Kerrera gradients'. However, he didn't want to invite the laird of Dunolly's displeasure by tactlessly making him aware that his established ferry had been bypassed by the illustrious visitors, so they had to make do without Dunolly's hospitality.

Until the introduction of mechanically-propelled craft well into the twentieth century, the boats used on the 'short' ferry crossing had to be capable of being rowed while being broad enough to accommodate a number of cattle as well as a number of passengers. Such a boat was the 28-ft long, 8-ft broad rowing craft shown in the 1935 photograph. She was probably built specially for the purpose by the Dunolly Estate. Once an engine-driven launch, usually 20 ft long, was introduced, the boat could be slim enough to achieve maximum speed with the greatest fuel economy and yet have space sufficient for passengers on routine ferry runs. The beamy cattle boat was now reserved for occasional use only, and she could be towed by the passenger launch, or sometimes even by an auxiliary 12-ft dinghy driven by an outboard engine. In 1973 the cattle boat being used was an ex-*Mauritania* lifeboat.

The 1935 ferry (loaned by Miss H. MacDougall of MacDougall)

Keith Runton at the helm of the *Christa*, towing the Campbeltown-built *Atlas*

Each beast was usually eased onto such a boat by its forelegs and pushed from behind.

Ian Beaton, who was the ferryman from 1953 to 1969, and who, in retirement, lived in Little Horseshoe Bay on the island, told of an 18-ft passenger launch and a 12-ft outboard dinghy he used to run in conjunction with the ex-*Mauritania* lifeboat. My memory of that 18-ft passenger launch dates from a family camping holiday, probably in a field belonging to Gallanachbeg Farm, quite close to the ferry jetty. One day, our party of some ten people of all ages was bound for Kerrera. The launch, with seating for well over twenty, already had at least twelve passengers on board. I knew that the launch had no passenger certificate, and therefore was not allowed to carry more than twelve persons. Not wanting to be an accomplice in lawbreaking, I impressed on my party the propriety of waiting about half an hour for the ferry to return empty, when our party of ten could be ferried across legally.

The launch returned, and having paid our fares, we spread ourselves over the boat's seating, but there was no sign of imminent departure. 'Are you going to take us across?' I asked the ferryman. 'It wouldn't be worth my while going with just a few of you,' came the reply. 'I'll wait and see if I can fill the boat before I go across.' Trying to look like an innocent passenger, I asked: 'You have a Board of Trade certificate for that number, of course?' The ferryman looked at me with condescension reserved for naïve strangers: 'I am the Board of Trade here,' he said slowly.

Ian Beaton, who died in 2002, was succeeded by Ned Rimmer and Keith Runton, during whose times the passenger ferry boats had to be replaced twice after having been lost in gales. The ex-*Mauritania* lifeboat was replaced

Maise, one of the *Lylen Lady*'s first passengers (loaned by Duncan MacEachan)

by a 25-ft steel landing craft for carrying cattle, built at Campbeltown shipyard. The passenger boat lost was one of character; she was *Mandy*, a 22-ft east coast salmon fishing coble with a high rising bow and a square low transom and propeller working in a semi-tunnel. She was acquired in 1987 by Keith Runton from Tom Brunton of Pennygael Mull, who had her for fishing. That passenger boat was replaced by an 18-ft aluminium alloy, riveted ex-army assault craft. Any water which came on board drained into a shallow double bottom space, to serve as ballast and improve the craft's stability.

Since 1999 the ferry is being run by Duncan MacEachen, who was born and brought up on Ardachoirc farm on Kerrera. He is still a tenant of the Dunollie Estate but owns the *Lylen Lady*, the present ferry. She is a 30-ft steel landing craft, built in 1999 at the Corpach boatyard in Fort William and powered by twin Honda 50 h.p. outboard engines. The vessel can carry twelve passengers, or 100 lambs or one car, provided it is 'island owned'.

Of late, the Oban–Lismore 'Island' class vehicular ferry (see Chapter 9) has been calling at the Ardantrive slip on odd occasions to carry commercial traffic. Occasional attempts at bringing in tourist traffic by the same means have not been successful at the time of writing.

9

LISMORE AND LOCH CRERAN

Lismore

The island of Lismore is about ten miles long and at no point more than two miles wide. It lies roughly along the centre line of the Firth of Lorn as it merges with Loch Linnhe.

Lismore is so much at the geometric centre of northern Argyll that the approximate shortest distances from it to the surrounding shores are: Appin three-quarters of a mile, Benderloch one mile, Mull one and a half miles, Kingairloch two miles and Lorn four miles. No wonder then that for many years Lismore possessed the Cathedral of the Isles. Communication over short and sheltered distances by sea was easier, and probably safer, than by land.

The shortest ferry crossing is to Port Appin in Benderloch from the north end of Lismore, and this has been the principal ferry route to the mainland for a very long time, but other crossings came into use as necessity arose. I came across the earliest mention of that ferry in the seventeenth-century *Minutes of the Synod of Argyll,* which noted that the Kirk services at Appin were disrupted in 1643 when the ferryman refused to transport the minister over from Lismore.

According to a record of 1752, the ferry was not properly established and regulated at that time, and that created problems:

> John Campbell, proprietor of the lands of Fiart on the island of Lismore, complained that soldiers of the garrison of Duart on Mull press the inhabitants of Fiart into ferrying them to Mull. He asks for an Act of the Commissioners of Supply for Argyll establishing a regular ferry, specifying freights and appointing harbours and quays to be made.

There were more problems in 1766, when the heritors (parish landholders) of Lismore petitioned on the subject of the disordered state of the ferry between Lismore and Appin, regarding a long-standing grievance. The ferryman sometimes ferried across to Kingairloch and was detained there. Captain Campbell of Achuaran on Lismore proposed to put up a new ferry boat and build a public house at a point in Achuaran nearly a mile away from the nearest private or public house. However, Donald Campbell of the Airds Estate, Appin, claimed exclusive rights to the ferry.

In spite of these problems, the ferry settled into reasonable stability over the next hundred years, the Lorn District Commissioner reporting in 1832 that two boats and two men were operating from Port Appin.

In 1874, Dougald MacFarlane signed a contract with the Airds Estate, Appin, which owned the ferry rights and the ferry boats. The ferryman undertook to pay an annual rent of £3 for the ferry and £2 for the ferry house at Port Appin, payable half-yearly. He was to pay a quarter of the cost of repairing the large ferry boat – presumably the one for the carriage of cattle – and 10s per year interest on its value. To the smaller boat – presumably the one for the carriage of passengers – he was to contribute 10 per cent of the craft's value in annual interest. For assisting the piermaster at the steamboat pier, he was to receive a yearly wage of £8, paid in equal portions at Martinmas and Whitsunday. He was not allowed to keep a gun or a dog. The proprietor and his family were to be carried free of charge. The contract document, signed by Dougald, is in elegant handwriting.

The Lismore ferry fares at the time were 6d per passenger, 9d for a horse, 3s for a boatload of household furniture and 6s for a four-wheeled carriage.

Both Dougald MacFarlane's wife and his daughter, Jessie Helen, helped with the boat, Jessie in particular working as ferry crew. The ferry house at Port Appin was a refuge for passengers to Lismore who were prevented by weather from crossing and would not or could not afford to stay at the Port Appin Hotel. Dougald went on ferrying until he was well into his seventies. In the end, he had to give up on his wife's insistence. She had a fright one

Dougald MacFarlane (loaned by Miss Janet Thomson)

night when, on the return passage from Lismore, the ferry was swept down the Sound of Lorn by the wind and the tide. Although retired from the ferry, Dougald remained the right-hand man of the Appin piermaster, Sandy Maclaughlan. Sandy came from a family settled on the tiny Eilean nan Caorach ('Sheep Island') at the north-eastern tip of Lismore, who worked lime there. Dougald died in 1923 in his late seventies.

Jessie Helen Macfarlane married into the Thomsons of Point House, Lismore. Her brother-in-law, Alexander Thomson, operated a ferry from Lismore at the same time as her brother, Alexander MacFarlane, was running the ferry to Lismore in succession to his father. The ferryman from the island was then tenant to the Revd Jos. Fell of Lismore.

Jessie, who spent most of her life about the boats which she loved, spun many a 'ferry tale' to her daughter, Janet, who kindly recounted some to me. This one is from the days when her father was the Port Appin ferryman.

> During one winter storm, Doctor Mackay of Appin was summoned to Lismore by a telegram from a lady on the island to the effect that she was dying. The doctor, who was an experienced boatman, consulted Dougald, and between them they decided to risk the crossing under the circumstances. When the doctor eventually got to the Lismore lady's bedside, she told him in Gaelic that she had enough wind in her stomach to sail a boat from Lismore to Kingairloch. Doctor Mackay was not amused, and he asked the Lismore postmistress to use more discretion in phrasing telegrams to him in the future.

Dougald with his daughter Jessie Helen (loaned by Miss Janet Thomson)

A ferryman with his lady (loaned by Miss Janet Thomson)

The old ferry house at Port Appin (loaned by Miss Janet Thomson)

The pier house, Port Appin (loaned by Miss Janet Thomson)

Jessie Helen Thomason died in Port Appin in 1978 aged 88. Soon after, Argyll County Council took over the Port Appin–Lismore Point ferry. A 28-ft wooden, clinker-planked motorboat was built for the service at Crinan Boatyard around 1970, similar to the one built for the Gigha ferry. That boat suffered occasional damage while in the charge of a county council ferryman who sometimes forgot to secure it overnight against wind and tide.

The ferrymen at the time of writing are Jim and John Thomson, still based at Port Appin. They run a 35-ft long steel, passenger-only ferry boat called the *Lismore* between piers constructed in the early 1980s. The *Lismore* was built in 1988 at Mills Boatyard, Whiteinch, Glasgow, at the reputed cost of £85,000.

Caledonian MacBrayne now also runs an 'Island' class steel vehicular ferry from Oban to Achnacroish in the centre of Lismore. There was a long and costly investigation, first by Argyll County Council and then by Strathclyde Region, into which end of the island the ferry should run to. The debate has not died with the establishment of the Oban–Achnacroish link and will no doubt go on, particularly on the island. Would the vehicular ferry benefit the islanders most if it ran from the point at the north end, where the crossing is shortest and where most crofters live, instead of the present southern route, over a longer distance, but linking to the metropolis of Oban and its railhead? It seems that the islanders would like a ferry at the north end capable of taking at least two cars or one small lorry, or a reasonable number of sheep or cattle, instead of having to make special arrangements for carrying cattle. They maintain that suitable facilities could be provided at a modest cost, whereas regional council plans tend to be grandiose and are repeatedly ruled out on grounds of expense. They remind people that as long ago as 1909, the

County Ferries Committee recommended that there should be a cattle boat on the Appin-Lismore crossing.

A story told by Adam Livingstone, a distant relative of the present Baron of Bachuill, Alaistair Livingstone, is maybe relevant here. As a young boy, he used to visit his relatives for holidays in Lismore. They bred heavy Clydesdale horses, which were taken off the island to be put up for sale. Of course, it was possible to swim them across the narrows at the north end, but this left them shivering and distressed. The solution was to take them across in a flatbottomed boat with a very low freeboard, which had been designed for the purpose. There was one further problem, however. Before they embarked, each horse had to be induced to stale (urinate), otherwise the liquid produce of four giant horses could reduce stability to the point of capsizing.

Loch Creran

Only two or three miles south of Port Appin, the ferry between North Shian in Appin and South Shian in Benderloch, crossing the mouth of Loch Creran, used to save passengers a fifteen-mile road journey between Oban and Fort William. The alternative, shorter Creagan crossing, half-way up Loch Creran, used to save only about half that distance.

The two ferries, the longer crossing at Shian and the shorter one at Creagan, had a mixed history, and to judge by such records as are available, not a very high reputation. Both left so much to be desired that in the eighteenth century, the Argyll Road Trustees tried to replace them with one at a different location. In 1803, Dorothy Wordsworth was anything but complimentary about the quality of the Shian ferry and the amenity of the ferryman's house. She would not trust the ferry boat with her horse and she nearly lost him while afloat. In the end, she was so glad to be on the other side that she tipped the ferryman with 1s 6d worth of whisky. Lord Cockburn was equally unimpressed with the Shian ferry: on his arrival, he was particularly angered by finding the ferry boat on the wrong side, despite the fact he had booked it. He thought a speedy crossing there would have been more of a miracle than the parting of the Red Sea. On another occasion in 1845, he managed to cross by the Creagan passenger ferry, but was again angered by having to leave his carriage behind.

In spite of all this, there must have been sufficient demand for the Shian ferry in the nineteenth century to warrant building an inn on either side. In 1832, the Lorn District Ferry Committee reported that Shian had two ferry boats and two men employed, 'with additional assistance in stormy weather'. With the appearance of the Oban railway line, passengers bound for Appin got off the train at Connel and were taken by coach to South Shian for the crossing to Appin.

A railway bridge was built across Loch Creran at the Creagan narrows in 1902, thus doing away with the Creagan ferry. Until 1965, the Ballachulish branch of the Oban railway ran across Loch Creran, with stations at Benderloch, Creagan and Appin. From then on, the use of the Shian ferry was restricted to local traffic, tourists and tinkers.

The quality and the efficiency of the Shian ferry have been variable into the twentieth century. In 1910, a letter was received by the Lorn District Ferry Committee asking them to take notice of the scandalous condition of the boats at Shian ferry: 'The boat on the beach at South Shian is broken and unfit to be launched. The boat at North Shian is not much better, the planks are so rotten and cracked that constant bailing is necessary to keep it afloat. It can only be taken out in smooth water.' On several occasions, the petitioner, who had to use the ferry frequently, had to turn back, hunt for a boat among the farmers and ferry himself across.

The service was not much better by 1914, although the fare went up to 1s per passenger. Travellers were advised to write in advance to North Shian, as there was no ferry station on the south side. The last ferryman at North Shian was Hugh Ross, whom I visited at the North Shian ferry house in 1985. He told me of a motorboat of 18 ft length and 5 ft beam which he ran from 1940 to 1948, when the service came to an end. The motor ferry carried sheep, calves and pigs or twelve passengers, and it took five minutes to cross. Before 1940, the crossing was made by rowing boats, and it took twelve minutes. There were then two rowing boats at North Shian. The 15-ft boat was larch-planked and very lightly built by Smith's of Tighnabruaich, where it cost £15, including delivery. The 12-ft boat was very heavy, and had been built at Arisaig. The 15-ft boat took twelve passengers, and the 12-ft boat eleven people, at a pinch. Rowing across Loch Creran could be heavy going, particularly with a north wind and a tide going east to west.

During the early part of Hugh's service, Donald Black worked a ferry from South Shian, and there were four rowing boats on the crossing altogether. In the later years of his service, he had to work the ferry on his own, and passengers at South Shian had to wave a flag in daytime to attract his attention; for a night crossing, they had to book ahead. There were no night crossings at all during the Second World War.

Mrs Mary MacArthur, who lived at Port Appin, a gracious lady of no mean age and with no mean knowledge of local history, told me that when she was a child her home was next door to the North Shian ferry house. She used to walk to South Shian from her school at Benderloch and then be ferried across. She enjoyed being rowed by Donald Black, who was a happy man, but she had to bail out the whole time. She used to wonder how he would manage to get back to South Shian with no one to bail for him. She did not need to bail Hugh Ross's boat.

10
LOCH AWE

Portsonachan

The Portsonachan ferry ran between Portsonachan (Port of Peace) on the east side of Loch Awe and Taycreggan on the west side (now the site of a hotel), a distance of some 570 yards. It was once part of the 'Road to the Isles'. Cattle from the Western Isles and from around Oban were ferried across on their way to the big markets at Crieff and Falkirk. However, since the Pass of Brander and the north part of Glen Nant might have been a difficult course for droving, the possibility arises of some droves not heading for the Portsonachan ferry. In such case they might have been proceeding from Dunollie through Brochroy, south-east to Fanans, on to Shellachan and Barrachander at the lower part of Glen Nant and then round Loch Tromlee to Ardnasaig and to a possible ferry across the mouth of River Awe, from Tervine to the north shore in the vicinity of the present power station. From there the drove route would lead along the north shore of Loch Awe and along River Orchy to Dalmally and onwards.

The place-name of Ardnasaig may have an association with a ferry to the island of Inishail (originally Innis Haile), where there is believed to have been a convent from the sixth century onwards, probably used also as an inn by passing travellers. From the thirteenth century until the Reformation there remained on the island the active church of St Findoc.

The Portsonachan ferry's legendary history dates back to the fourteenth century. From the earliest times, there were hereditary ferrymen on Loch Awe, the MacPhedrans of Portsonachan, just as there were hereditary boatbuilders, the MacIllchonells. According to tradition, Sir Neil Campbell, the laird of Loch Awe, who was a trusted friend and supporter of King Robert the Bruce and who died in 1315, granted the lands and ferry rights to a MacPhedran.

The story goes that on one occasion, Sir Neil had a large muster of his galleys on Loch Awe. Suddenly, a storm blew up and he saw with alarm that the galley carrying his son, Duncan, was in danger of sinking. He appealed to a MacPhedran, who with skilful manoeuvring succeeded in bringing Duncan's storm-beaten galley to a safe haven. In gratitude, Sir Neil granted to the MacPhedran the lands of Portsonachan on the east side of Loch Awe, with ferrying rights on that side and on the west side at 'Tigh-a-Chreagan' (Taychreggan) – 'Inn of the rocks'. The MacPhedrans held those lands and rights for hundreds of years.

The MacPhedran family papers tell of 'the great and honest man Moricius MacFedren' having presented a paper of 1439 in which 'Duncan Cambel' of Loch Awe granted to 'Dominicus McFederane' the lands of Portsonachan along with the duty of ferrying. For this, Dominicus was to 'pay thence yearly ten shillings of silver, two balls[1] of grain which is called barley and oats, one pound of cheese and a sheep'. Furthermore, Dominicus was to carry all infirm, lame or blind passengers across the loch without charge. This was verified by two charters from the earls of Argyll in 1501 and 1590.

The last of the family in possession of the land and ferry, according to one tradition, was Donald McGillemore MacPhedran, who, having no sons, disposed of Portsonachan in 1627 in favour of his friend and neighbour, Duncan Campbell of Sonachan. It has been said that when Duncan tried to take possession of the little property upon MacPhedran's death, he and his two sons were set upon by the earl of Argyll's party and killed. The earl was apparently convinced that, as the superior, the land and ferry should have fallen to him. The cairns above Portsonachan Hotel may be the graves of Duncan and his sons.

This story tallies with the record of the Marquess of Argyll giving the feu of the land and the ferry rights of Portsonachan to Ian Campbell of Dunstaffnage in 1656. However, the rights were confined to a portion of Loch Awe, while the rights of the former feuers extended over the whole of it. The earl also imposed a heavy feu duty on Dunstaffnage, with the servitude of ferrying the family of Argyll, their servants, horses and all lame and blind, paupers and foreigners without any ferry charge.

However, this tradition conflicts with the story told by John MacIntyre, one-time sexton of Kilchrenan. According to his version, the MacPhedrans' tenure of Portsonachan ended only in 1706, in an encounter between them and the Campbells of Sonachan, when the latter claimed the rights to the ferry dues. The battle took place at a burn half-way between Sonachan House and the present Portsonachan Hotel, and the Campbells, with the assistance of four neighbouring clans, overpowered the MacPhedrans. Thus the famous breed of Loch Awe sailors became dispossessed and scattered. Some of the MacPhedrans settled by Loch Fyne, where they flourished and were noted for producing sea captains and pipers.

Until well into the eighteenth century, the state of 'Leckan Muir' (Leacann Muir, the hilly moorland between Loch Fyne and Loch Awe) was such that men crossing it to approach the ferry from the east could move faster than horses. A seventeenth-century legend tells of a MacKellar, the foster

---

1 A variant spelling of 'boll' (see the Glossary).

brother of Campbell of Dunstaffnage, outrunning horses from Inveraray to Portsonachan ferry. Colquitto, Lieutenant of Montrose, took a long time crossing here when Inveraray was about to be sacked in 1645. Later in the eighteenth century, the route to and from the ferry became more accessible as cattle droving increased, and Taycreggan – Portsonachan became the drovers' principal crossing point of Loch Awe. Rob Roy MacGregor was reputed to have used the ferry to convey his beasts, and in 1745, so did a messenger bearing the news of Prince Charles Stewart's landing in Scotland.

During the Jacobite Rebellion, the ferry played its part in transporting government soldiers to and fro, but even before 1745, work was in progress on the military road between Inveraray and Tyndrum (now the A819) and the Commissioners of Supply for Argyll were hoping to benefit through army labour being used to improve the eastern approach to the Portsonachan ferry. In 1759, some thought was even being given to moving the ferry further north, nearer Cladich on the Inveraray–Tyndrum road, and to making short access roads on both sides of the loch to connect with the new ferry location.

This project having been abandoned, Campbells of Stonefield and of Airds were asked to map out a road from Cladich to Portsonachan. Some work was done under the direction of Campbell of Sonachan, but it did not get as far as building the necessary road bridges until the 1770s. Doctor Johnson and James Boswell, having crossed by the ferry in 1773, had to wade through flooded fords to Cladich.

In the 1770s a Campbell of Dunstaffnage petitioned the Argyll Commissioners to fund repairs to the Portsonachan quay, to put the ferry freights on the same footing as those of the Bonawe and Connel ferries on Loch Etive (see Chapter Eleven) and to abolish the practice of ferry payments being tendered in corn and other articles. This was agreed, but the inhabitants of Kilchrenan were to be allowed a 50 per cent reduction in fares. The agreed fares were: saddle horse and rider or pedlar and horse 4d, foot passenger 2d, and a four-wheeled chaise with two horses 3s 6d. In 1798, Neil Campbell of Dunstaffnage tried unsuccessfully to have the fares increased, but they remained unaltered till 1813. In 1800, the advice from Ronaldson, Surveyor to the Deputy Postmaster General of Scotland, was to avoid the Portsonachan ferry.

In the early 1800s, Robert Campbell of Sonachan bought the superiority and feu of the ferry from the 5th duke of Argyll, which made him a direct tenant of the Crown at the annual rent of 1d Scots.

The advent of steamer services on the west coast of Scotland in the first quarter of the nineteenth century had the secondary effect of reducing the Loch Awe ferry traffic, despite a mail ferry coming into service on the route and Portsonachan coming within the scope of the Kilchrenan penny post. Then 1830 saw a lengthy confrontation between Robert Campbell of

Sonachan and the Lorn District Road Trustees, who wanted to reduce the ferry fares and who, Robert thought, had no jurisdiction over him, his ferry being in the district of Mid-Argyll, not Lorn. He thought the ferry was overvalued, since all the tenants had gone bankrupt for lack of traffic, and in the end he had to run the ferry himself. The average rent of the ferry, when let, was stated to be £25 10s.

The 1840 attempt by Campbell of Inverawe, convener of the Portsonachan Ferry Committee, to install a ferry boat on the west side of the loch in addition to the two boats on the east side, came to nothing because the District Trustees would not provide a space in which to keep it. New standards for the ferry introduced during the 1840s included the requirement for two rails, with the upper one 3 ft above the gunwale, and for a small, 16-ft long boat of 5 ft beam to be kept for the benefit of passengers who preferred not to share the ferry boat with horses. It was also conceded that the freight for a whole load of household furniture could be more than 2s.

In the 1840s, a curious incident occurred. Duncan MacGregor, schoolmaster of Kilchrenan, who was also the local Collector of Poor Rates, boarded the ferry boat at 4 a.m. with a bag of account books which were to be audited that day (his honesty was apparently being questioned). While in passage, Duncan fell into the loch, losing all the account books in its depths.

The Malcolms of Poltalloch, who bought the Sonachan Estate in 1850, built the present Portsonachan Hotel, and in 1873 they installed Thomas Cameron as tenant. He took over the ferry boat, valued, with two oars and chains, at £42 11s.

The 1891 *Schedule of Ferries* shows how the fares slowly crept up: a full-sized, four-wheeled carriage was now charged 5s, an 'entire horse' (i.e. ungelded) 1s, a bull 8d and a single passenger 4d. There were two boats, one large and one small, based at Portsonachan. The 1909 *Report of the Argyll County Council's Ferry Committee* still refers to two boats: a small one with one pair of oars for passengers only, and a large, beamy one, 22 ft by 10 ft, capable of carrying horses, cattle and even carriages. The official scale of fares was much the same, with the addition of a bicycle fare at 6d, but the tenant and ferry operator, Thomas Cameron, did not think he was bound by it at all times, and felt he should not be expected to take out his big boat for under 2s, as two men were required to row it. In the summer, the big boat was generally towed by his steamer, the *Caledonia*. The boats were kept at the Portsonachan pier, which was maintained by Lorn District Council as part of the highway system. The ferryman's house was close to the pier. In Thomas Cameron's times, the Portsonachan ferryman was a MacIntyre of Mull.

The increase in motor traffic after the First World War had a further adverse effect on the demand for ferrying across Loch Awe, and a deterioration in the standard of service followed. Mrs Thorpe of Ardbrecknish complained to the

Taycreggan from Portsonachan (loaned by the Scottish Ethnological Archive)

county council in 1921 that 'there was only one small rowing boat available and that the ferryman is more often absent than present'. The district nurse, who was resident in Kilchrenan, had often whistled for the ferry for an hour or more when summoned to a case on the east side of the loch, and she had been compelled to give up trying to attend. Dr McNicol also suffered serious delays. No redress could be obtained in response to complaints addressed to Miss Cameron at the Portsonachan Hotel, who inherited the ferry contract.

The ferry was struck by a misfortune in 1946, the year Colonel James Young bought the hotel, together with the ferrying rights, when the ferryman, Charles Livingstone, was tragically drowned. In 1953, Colonel Young requested the county council's permission to discontinue the service. This was granted, and the Portsonachan ferry came to an end after five-and-a-half centuries of recorded history.

Portinnisherrich

Portinnisherrich is a bay about half-way up the east side of Loch Awe which forms a natural port and derives its name from the small island, Innis sèa-ràmhach ('Isle of the Six Oars', or 'Isle of the Six-Oared Galley'). This suggests that galleys in ancient times may have anchored in the bay, protected from westerly winds by the island. There is a late medieval chapel on the island.

in a burial ground which was in use until fairly recent times. A sixteenth-century map shows it as 'Incherry', and on the adjacent shore there was an inn, presumably for the benefit of the ferry travellers. New York (sometimes spelt 'Newyork'), the western terminal of the ferry, is derived from the name of the fraudulent eighteenth-century York Building Company, which bought the lochside lands forfeited after the 1715 Jacobite Rising.

The Portinnisherrich ferry formed a vital link in the drove road system from early times. A drove route from the west coast via Loch Avich crossed Loch Awe to Portinnisherrich, ran south to Durran and then across Leacann Muir to Auchindrain on Loch Fyne. The same route was perhaps followed, in the opposite direction, in pre-medieval times by funeral cortèges heading for Iona, using Carraig nan Marbh ('Rock of the Dead') in Loch Feochan, south of Oban, as a pier.

In 1571, a charter was granted by Archibald, the fifth earl of Argyll, in favour of Ian Dow MacGeillreid MacKachray, 'to be holden in free alms for ever, conform to ancient mortification for annually upholding a ferry boat for the superiors' use when required, and for upholding the same for the common services of the Parishioners of Kilchrenan, they paying yearly nane to use and wont'.

Slightly to the north of Portinnisherrich lies the island of Innis Chonnell, with a castle which has been in the hands of the earls of Argyll since the times of Robert the Bruce. During the early part of the seventeenth century, the captain of the castle, who acted on behalf of the earl, was Donald MacLauchlane. He was granted rights over the ferry and those of 'malt and brewstery', which must have helped the ferry inn.

In the mid-seventeenth century, the ferry was of strategic importance. Following the Marquess of Montrose's successful attack on Inveraray in 1644, when he drove the 8th earl of Argyll from his castle, a force of soldiers from Inveraray used Portinnisherrich ferry as the shortest route in pursuit of Argyll's enemy. The Army of the Covenant crossed by the ferry a year later, when they marched from Edinburgh to Argyll to defeat Alasdair McColla in Kintyre.

The ferry prospered throughout the eighteenth century, partly because, prior to the opening of the Crinan Canal in 1801, travellers to the west coast found the land route less perilous than sailing round the Mull of Kintyre. Ferry boats became large enough to carry not only cattle driven from the Western Isles to the markets of central Scotland, but also horses and carriages. How the value of the ferry had risen by the mid-century can be judged from the £60 rent Donald Campbell, the 'tacksman of Innissherick', agreed to pay. The ferry traffic increased to such an extent that the road across Leacann Muir, between Durran on Loch Awe and Auchindrain on Loch Fyne, too steep in places for wheeled carriages, came to be considered inadequate, and surveys were undertaken for a road crossing the moor to a point closer to the ferry than Durran.

The reason why the new road did not materialise can be traced to the rapid expansion of steamer traffic in the 1820s, which made travellers forsake the overland route. A new road was not built in these parts until 1870, when the Malcolms of Poltalloch commissioned one the length of the east side of Loch Awe, from Ford to Portsonachan, to join up the Loch Aweside estates they gradually acquired, starting with Portinnisherrich, which they bought, with ferry rights, around 1830. No improved road across Leacann Muir to connect the ferry with Loch Fyne was ever built, the only route between Loch Fyne and Loch Awe suitable for vehicular traffic remaining the Glen Aray road from Inveraray to Cladich. Most of the old road between Durran and Auchindrain is shown on today's Ordnance Survey maps as a footpath.

The Malcolms' factor requested the closure of the ferry in 1870. There were protests from Dalavich and other townships on Loch Aweside, until John MacIntyre of Newyork took on the ferry for £10 per year. The General Road Trustees contributed £5 per annum, on the understanding that the Mid-Argyll District Road Trustees would contribute the same.

The 1891 *Schedule of Particulars as to Ferries* refers to the Portinnisherrich ferry as 'active'. However, John MacIntyre died in 1902, and the 1909 *Report of Argyll County Council's Road Committee* stated that because the Boundary Commission had transferred the ferry to Lorn District, which discontinued the ferryman's allowance, the ferry was no longer worked regularly.

11
LOCH ETIVE

Connel

For centuries, Connel ferry has straddled the narrows at the mouth of Loch Etive, linking Benderloch with Lorne. In the seventeenth century, the ferry was put 'under caution' by the Privy Council because of suspected complicity in the traffic in stolen cattle. The narrowness and sunken rocks at the site of the ferry crossing, a geological feature resulting from glacial action known as a 'fjord step', cause turbulence, particularly at ebb tide. The tide-race, known locally as the Falls of Lora, has always been a headache for ferrymen, but in 1799, Sarah Murray wrote that the ferry boats at Connel were being turned round in perfect safety. In the same period, John Stoddart wrote of how entertaining it was to behold the dextrous navigation of small boats skirting the edge of the whirlpool. He thought Connel ferry was safer than many.

Later, the complaints were mainly about the small size of ferry boats, which meant that horses sometimes had to be towed astern or alongside. John MacCulloch wrote to Sir Walter Scott: 'He who comes to Connel Ferry will require a large share of patentia ferryboatica as a Highland horse does not choose to take his seat in a boat.' Dorothy Wordsworth was not uncritical of Connel ferry: the horse 'was in terror before he reached the boat', and the ferryman 'completed the work by beating him and pushing him by main force over the ridge of the boat'. During the passage, 'the men were swearing terrible oaths', and when they reached the landing place, 'they whipped him ashore in brutal triumph'.

A new quay was built at Connel in the 1820s for £118 15s, but no ferry boat was kept on that side, and in 1832, Donald Campbell of Dunstaffnage petitioned the Lorn District Road Trustees for one to be stationed on the south side of the ferry, at Connel. He argued that the rapidity of the current and the prevailing southerly gales often rendered it impracticable to bring the boat across from the north side, 'whereas a free communication can at all times be expected from the South'. Travellers arriving at the south side in the evening and unable to make themselves heard were obliged to proceed nearly five miles out of their way to Oban to find lodgings for the night. In response to the petition, the Road Trustees decreed in favour of boats being kept on the south side. The ferry inn remained on the north side, and it is still there, now a hotel.

The 1846 scale of fares at Connel ferry, as decided by the Commissioners of Supply and the justices of the peace sitting at Inveraray, was: wheeled carriages drawn by four horses 6s, heifers and stirks 4d each, cart and horse loaded 2s 6d, cart and horse empty 2s, foot passengers 3d. The Rules for the Conveyance of Parcels across the ferry of half a century later stipulated personal luggage allowance of 28 lbs or two cubic feet in bulk. One penny to be charged for every 28 lbs or part thereof in excess of that amount. For heavier goods one penny to be charged for every hundredweight!

I came across several letters complaining about the behaviour of North Connel ferrymen dating to 1890. Mr Rainy, an Edinburgh gentleman, missed the morning train from Connel ferry station because the ferry men refused to get him across in good time. He wrote 'surely forty minutes is an excessive time to waste at the ferry when crossing can easily be made in ten minutes'. Mr Calder Macphail, another Edinburgh gentleman, wrote directly to the laird, Robert Macfie of Airds, relating the unfortunate experience of his youngest daughter and her two girlfriends while crossing southwards in order to catch a train. The weather was rough and the single boatman was tipsy and unable to manage the boat alone: 'He fell off his seat, dropped an oar overboard and my daughter had to take one of the oars.' Back on the north side the drunken ferryman attacked the waiting coach because his demand for an extra halfpenny was met with a penny. Mr MacPhail suggested that the ferry-houses on both sides should no longer be licensed to sell intoxicating liquor since there was now a respectable hotel at North Connel owned by the ferry lessee.

After the Connel railway bridge was completed in 1903, cars, drained of petrol, were at first transported by rail, while passengers still used the ferry. In 1909, the factor of the Loch Nell Estate let it be known that, owing to the competition of the railway company, he had no intention of taking up the working of the North Connel ferry for motor traffic during the winter months, unless he had a guaranteed payment.

Just before the First World War, the track across the bridge alongside the railway line became a toll bridge available to motor cars and pedestrians when no trains were due. It was only in the 1960s, when the Ballachulish railway line fell to the Beeching axe, that the bridge became fully open and toll-free to motor traffic, and the ferry faced closure.

Bonawe

Loch Etive is a formidable barrier. Bonawe ferry, to the east of Connel, crossing 370 yards of the loch, was, like Connel, situated where the drove roads from the west and north met. Generations of travellers from Glen Etive in the north-east, through Glen Salach from Benderloch and Appin in the west and from the grim Pass of Brander in the east, found themselves funnelled into the narrows of 'Bunaw' (Bun Atha, 'or Mouth of the River Awe', now spelt 'Bonawe') in order to continue their journey. The iron works established on the south side of the loch in the flood plain of the River Awe at Bonawe in the mid-eighteenth century increased the importance of the crossing, and when the Bonawe Quarry, on the north side of the loch, opened in the 1880s, the road from the north leading to the ferry was improved with local labour.

In the nineteenth century, the ferry prospered and, according to the 1891 *Schedule of Particulars* and the 1909 *Report of the Ferry Committee*, operated with one large and two small boats, and at least two ferrymen. The operators were tenants of the Campbell-Prestons of Ardchattan Priory. The large boat belonged to the proprietor, and the small ones to the tenant, all of them being rowing boats. The large boat had a capacity of 3 tons and was not big enough to carry motor cars when they appeared on the scene. Just before the First World War, a 10-ton boat was introduced, capable of carrying cars.

Lachie MacKinnon of Coll, who worked on the ferry in the 1930s and '40s and lives in retirement in Kilchrenan at the time of writing, tells of the 20-ft by 8-ft rowing 'cattle' ferry, built at Connel, which used to have a crew of four men handling square oars. He remembers the turntable car ferry being introduced in the late 1930s by the owners of the ferry, J. & A. Gardner, and being taken away by them during the Second World War. It was returned after the end of hostilities. It was a beam-loading vessel with a capacity of four cars, and it operated continuously between sloping piers. The ferry was in operation from 7.30 a.m. to 10.30 p.m., and the crew had only three holidays per year: Easter, Glasgow Fair and New Year. When ferrying lorries carrying building materials, the ferrymen had to start at 6.30 a.m. The ferry was under contract to the Post Office to carry mail to Bonawe. The Taynuilt 'postie' delivered the mail to the pier on a motorbike with a sidecar to accommodate the mailbags. When the need arose in Taynuilt for a quantity of Bonawe Quarry gravel, Lachie and his two mates thought nothing of filling twenty bags at the loading berth, rowing them across in the 'cattle' boat and shifting them on the other side. The 'cattle' ferry boat was sometimes also used for conveying coffins and mourners to burials at Ardchattan Priory.

Lachie was asked to join the crew of the ferry in the early 1930s by Mr MacGilvray of Iona, who was just taking over as the ferry skipper. Bob Scott was the ferryman before MacGilvray, and Lachie tells that on the day he left the ferry, Bob went to Taynuilt to catch the train for Dalmally, taking his dog with him. No sooner had Bob disappeared than a woman turned up wanting to be taken to the south side.

Inverawe

Lachie introduced himself as the new crew, and she asked suspiciously whether he knew anything about boats. On having been rowed to the other side, she said to Lachie: 'You may not know much about boats, but you are still a damned good rower.' Just as the woman disembarked, in jumped Bob Scott's dog, who, on arriving on the north side, went straight for the ferry house. Apparently, he had parted company with his master at Taynuilt station and decided to go home.

There were some hundred men working at Bonawe Quarry in those days, a built-in clientele for the ferry. Most of the Bonawe Quarry folk were Roman Catholics. They would cross by the ferry several times a week when masses were celebrated at the Roman Catholic chapel in Taynuilt, and there were special ferry crossings during the six weeks of Lent.

Many of those who lived on the north shore would cross on the evening ferry for a visit to the Taynuilt Hotel. On their way back, they used to shout across the loch, although the recognised way of attracting the ferry from the Taynuilt side was to flash an electric torch at the ferry house. Anne Macfarlane remembers quarrymen already starting to shout 'Boo-a-t' at Brochroy, a good distance from the ferry. A persistent offender in this respect was one Jimmy Holland, who used to start shouting even before he reached the little hill at the chapel. The quarrymen used to stop hopefully, but misguidedly, before the name-plate of her mother's house, which said 'Tigh-nam-barr'. Sometimes, a quarryman could be found asleep on the ferry when she was about to start up in the morning. On one occasion, one of these nightly passengers, Tom Kelly, was making his way from the hotel, carrying a quantity of liquid refreshment on him. He slipped and fell on the pier as he was about to board the boat. When Lachie helped him up, Tom whispered anxiously that he had a bottle in his pocket. Lachie investigated, and Tom was very pleased to learn that what was running down his trouser leg was blood, not whisky!

It was not unusual for the ferry to transport flour in 140 lb bags. A big woman passenger once boarded the ferry and sat down, hitching up her skirts. Lachie greeted her with: 'My, you are some weight!' The lady had unguardedly exposed her knickers made out of flour bags, each leg of which was branded '140 lbs'.

One summer, when MacGilvray was in hospital in Glasgow, Lachie went on ferrying for three nights without going to bed. Each night, he had to go to Taynuilt station to meet the 4 a.m. mail train bringing the first batch of Glasgow Fair holidaymakers of the day. Another time, Lachie was left in charge after MacGilvray's motorbike collided with the schoolmaster's car while the skipper was on his way to collect his wife Sally MacGilvray, from an Ardchattan Priory Christmas party, to which she had been invited, having been a maid at the priory.

The only major ferry accident Lachie remembers was on the car ferry *Deirdre*, when a lorry went overboard after its brakes failed. The quarry engineer later congratulated Lachie on the fact that the lorry sank at the pier and not in deep water. As for the ferry, she hit the pier and holed herself. Lachie beached her for repairs, and he and his mate worked two days and two nights making a temporary patch on her.

In Lachie's time, the ferry fares were still 6d for a return adult crossing, 4d for a child's return and 6d for a horse, but there was now a 1s 6d fare for a motorbike, a 9d one for a passenger on a pushbike and a 3s fare for a car.

Lachie left the ferry for quarry employment in 1947, by which time the ferry traffic was already shrinking due to the reduced number of quarrymen as a result of mechanisation. MacGilvray was followed as ferry skipper by John Mackenzie, generally known as 'Hurricane Jeck'. In the 1948 *Review of Ferries*, no recommendation was made for the development of the Loch Etive vehicular ferry. In fact, the vehicular ferry was no longer needed from 1964, when Connel Bridge was fully opened for motor traffic and ceased to be a toll bridge. Sandy Black of Brochroy Farm ran the Loch Etive mail ferry service until the 1970s; he also used a fairly large motorboat to deliver goods to the houses and remote farms on the north shore.

Although the Bonawe ferry as such has long since ceased to run, it may be a consolation to know that, at the time of writing, a tourist ferry still leaves the narrows at the Taynuilt side daily in summer and takes goods and passengers to the isolated farms that lie in the headwaters of Loch Etive. A strategically-placed line of communication never loses its value.

Penny Ferry

This chapter would not be complete without mention of the ferry across the mouth of the River Awe, which was, until its closure, known by the older generation as the 'Penny Ferry'. This ferry, like the Bonawe ferry, lies on an ancient line of communication for travellers wishing to go east or west.

The eastern end of the ferry was served by an old inn known locally as 'Tign-na-h-Aibhne' ('River Inn'), situated on a shelf of land beside the river and sheltered by a venerable grove of elm and ash trees. It was here that MacDonald of Glencoe is said to have taken refuge on a snowy winter night late in 1691, delayed on his way south to Inveraray to enter into the King's Peace; the delay led to the Glencoe Massacre. Unfortunately, the inn was demolished in the late 1950s to make way for a service road to a hydroelectric installation – a sad fate for such a historic building.

Even within living memory, the inn, although no longer dispensing hospitality, was a sturdy building with stone-flagged floors, oak settles and a peat fire. The ferryman sheltered under a tree until called, and then rowed upstream so as to drift skilfully down to the landing place on the opposite bank. The earliest ferryman (and ferrywoman!) that can be recalled in the twentieth century were Duncan MacNicol and his sister, Catherine, who was a skilled oarswoman. She was known far and wide locally as 'Ceit na-h-Aibhne' ('Kate of the River') and would have been a familiar figure to the children from Inverawe who were scholars at Oban High School and would have made the crossing twice daily, once in the morning to catch the 'Scholars' Train' to Oban, and once on the return journey.

The MacNicols were followed by Donald MacBean, one of the old local family who had lost three sons in the First World War and who were traditionally connected with the 'Penny Ferry'. He was still plying his trade in 1952 and used to have a seat under an enormous ash tree beside the inn where he waited for people to shout 'Boat'. He was succeeded by a ferryman called MacGregor, who rejoiced in the nickname 'Right Oh Mac'. By that time, the fare had risen from 1d to 2s. The increase in car ownership, the start of the hydro-electric scheme at Inverawe and the improvement of the road from Inverawe to Bridge of Awe all lowered the usage of the ferry. A service which had for many centuries conveyed travellers quietly across the Awe estuary in the face of all weathers was overtaken by events and was obliged to close.

12
LOCH FYNE

Cairndow

Cairndow lies on the east shore of Loch Fyne, about a mile below the head of the loch. Dorothy Wordsworth, in her *Recollections of a Tour made in Scotland* in 1803 (published in 1974), writes of a ferry for foot passengers from Cairndow to the other side of Loch Fyne, which might have saved pedestrians a three-mile walk:

> While the road along which all carriages go is carried round the head of the loch perhaps a distance of 3 miles . . . The ferryboat was to be summoned from the opposite side to convey us over the water, our luggage (no great weight it is true) to be carried to the shore of the loch for embarkation . . . We must make our way as well as we could, with luggage in hand, to the Ferry Point, where, as the landlord said, we must shout, our wants would be understood on the other shore and the boat would come to us.

Creggans Ferry

Creggans ferry – later also known as Strachur ferry – used to run across Loch Fyne about two miles south-west of Inveraray.

When Colin Campbell, 1st earl of Argyll, granted the lands of Kibride in the parish of Glenaray to Duncan Campbell of Glenorchy in 1482, he kept in his own hands the 'half merkland of the Ferry of Cragane',[1] which had been an important point of crossing Loch Fyne from early times. The crossing of the loch between Wester Creggans and Port Creggan on the Strachur shore of Cowal is one of the shortest, and it had the advantage of leading along the Loch Eck road, directly to the important shrine at Kilmun on the Holy Loch.

It is said that the ancestors of the Argyll family had always stipulated that the vassal who held the ground at Creggans should ferry, without payment, all pilgrims, the halt and the blind. It was common for the vassals of the earl of Argyll to be required to provide transport across the many inlets of the sea.

---

1 The merkland was a unit of land value – see Glossary.

For example, the rent of Dunoon Castle in 1649 included 'a ship of 10 oars' as well as four bolls of barley and 27½ stones of cheese.

The history of Creggans ferry owes an early record to Mary, Queen of Scots, whose half-sister, Jean Stewart, was the wife of the 5th earl of Argyll. In July 1563, Mary, then aged twenty, made 'royal progress' to Inveraray as part of a journey which took her to Dunure Castle, Dumfries and Peebles. She enjoyed the scenery and the fine hunting. Her court included the earl of Moray and the chancellor of Scotland, the earl of Morton. All wore 'highland apparel' for the tour, and the English Ambassador, not to be outdone, fitted himself out 'in outer shape . . . like unto the rest'. Little has been recorded on her visit to Inveraray, but it is known that on Monday 26 July the royal party crossed Loch Fyne from Wester Creggans to Port Creggan, where they stayed at Castle Dreip, as guests of Urie Campbell of Strachur. They then proceeded to Dunoon, where they stayed for a further three days.

Miss Marion Campbell's poem 'Inveraray 1563' contains the following verse:

> Queen Mary rode down by Cowal,
> At Creggan Ferry the boats were braw,
> In the door o' the auld gray tower of Aors,
> Sister-countess loutit to sister-Queen.

The road taken by the royal party was later used extensively by local drovers from the early eighteenth century onwards. The Creggans crossing, like those at St Catherines and Otter Ferry (see below), was convenient for the Cowal route, with access via Loch Eckside to the Clyde coast at Dunoon and Ardentinny. Several thousands of black cattle were shipped annually to the southern markets this way.

According to Duke Niall's 1665 notebook, a feud arose at that time over the ownership of Creggans ferry lands. Ian MacPhune of Dreip alleged that he was the feuer of the lands of Creggans ferry, paying £40 a year for them. Donald MacKerris deposed that the lands were part of Argyll property, were never felled, and that the possessor had no right to them except that given by the former earl of Argyll for ferrying and keeping the boats, 'which ferry boats are well worth the fief'. In 1717, the Wester Creggans ferry was set in tack (leased) to Dugald Clerk of Braleckan for nineteen years, commencing Whitsunday, for £26 13s 4d.

The duke's instructions for John Campbell, chamberlain of Argyll, in 1740 were: 'let it be recommended to Gilmour to keep up the ferry at Creggans and to apply no freights for his own use, he keeping the boats in repair'. The valuation roll of the shire of Argyll compiled in 1751 for Archibald, the 3rd duke of Argyll, shows the rent of the half-merkland of Wester Creggans to be £1 5s. However by 1756 the rental of the Wester Creggans ferry had risen to

£90 Scots and appears to have been paid by 'Kentras heirs': it is possible that this was the fan-lily of the Campbells of Kintraw.

The Scots *Magazine* of September 1783 reported:

> On Saturday 23 August a very melancholy accident happened at Creagan Ferry about 2 miles to the Southward of Inveraray. Lt. Robert Campbell of the late 71st Regiment of Foot, brother to Dugald Campbell of Elderline, with his servant Archibald Leitch and their two horses, were crossing from the Cowal side to the Argyll side in the ferry boat which was manned by Duncan MacTavish and a man called Luke. The boat being an old one, and a very bad one for ferrying horses, was so constructed that both horses had to stand in the stern, which made it necessary to ballast the fore part with stones. When they were about a third way, or something more, across the Sound, a storm came on, which occasioned a swell of the sea. The horses jumped out of the boat, which heeled so much that she filled, and the stone ballast sunk her in an instant. Lt. Campbell and Luke held the mane of one of the horses, who made back for the Cowal side. When they approached the shore at a distance that Lt. Campbell thought he could make out by swimming, he dreading the horse might fag by the weight of two of them upon him, made shift to put off his sirtout [overcoat] and set off in his coat, boots etc. For some time he kept ahead of Luke and the horse, but about a pistol shot from the shore, he was so much spent that he got upon his back to rest himself, and lay in that position until Luke with the horse got ashore. Some old men about the ferryman's house, being appraised of what happened, went to his assistance with a yawl, into which they could not take Lt. Campbell but dragged him after her to shore. When the yawl came near him he took hold of the person's hand that catched him, but notwithstanding his being thus sensible when taken up and of every possible means being used for his recovery, in which the minister of Strachur and a physician from this town [presumably Inveraray] assisted, he expired about 10 o'clock that night.

In 1770, the Committee of Road Trustees for the Lorn District were of the opinion that at Creggans and the other two main Loch Fyne ferries, the freights ought to be: for a single man 6d; for two or more 3d each; for a man and a horse 9d; and the freight of sheep and black cattle 'should continue as formerly'. The proprietors were empowered and authorised to exact the freights at the ferries 'in all times coming'.

In 1822, the Creggans ferryman, Archibald Thomson, was cited by the Collector of Excise for Argyll to appear before the justices of the peace at Lochgilphead, charged with selling spirit without a licence. In his petition, the ferryman did not deny that he kept a little whisky for 'the accommodation and a little refreshment' of passengers using the ferry. He further pleaded that owing to the steamboats plying from the Clyde to Inveraray and in Loch Long to Lochgoilhead, 'the intercourse by Ardentinny, Strachur and across the Creggans ferry is almost entirely done away with'. Consequently, the petitioner had sold very little whisky for some years. 'On these accounts he would not be disposed to keep either the ferry or whisky were it not that the ferry is inseparably connected with the small farm he possesses. Upon these circumstances he humbly lays himself under the mercy and clemency of the justices of the Peace.'

Ferryman Thomson's circumstances tie up with earlier records in the old parish register relating to families living at Creggans in 1767. It seems that they were crofters and fishermen who ferried passengers when required. With the village around Creggans House thriving as a fishing and crofting community, its function changed from ferry house to schoolhouse. In the mid-nineteenth century, Elisabeth Turner, who had become the teacher at Creggans, received Creggans House and garden rent-free from the duke. When she retired in 1870, Duchess Elisabeth, wife of the 8th duke, began to look at Creggans School as her special interest. A splendid new schoolroom was added, and the two Miss Gibsons were appointed at a salary of £35 per year.

In spite of the parlous state of the ferry business bemoaned by the ferryman in the 1820s, according to the 1891 *Schedule of Particulars as to Ferries,* the ferry was still functioning. It was recorded that a sizeable boat, which was seldom required, was operated by Donald Campbell, innkeeper at Strachur, and that the pier was maintained by the Inveraray Steamboat Company. The innkeeper was bound to carry any party to the opposite side on payment of 1s per head. All goods were carried by the steamer calling at the Creggans, Inveraray and Furnace piers. The Inveraray Creggans Female School lasted into the twentieth century, but the building is now a private residence.

Brainport

Brainport ferry – also known as the 'chapel ferry' – operated between Brainport Point, near Minard on the west shore of Loch Fyne, and the small bay below Kilbride Chapel at Strathlachlan, on the east shore of the loch, a distance of 2¼ miles. On the east side, a slipway, which is still visible, had been cleared below the chapel site, where it was partly sheltered by Kilbride Island. On the Minard side, a similar slipway was cleared south of Brainport Point, where it is protected from the southerly gales by a ridge of rock. Several buildings associated with the running of the ferry were located here.

According to Colonel P. Fane Gladwin, one cannot be sure when the ferry began, but its association with the early Christian wayside chapel at Kilbride points to it having been in use before medieval times. On both sides of the loch, the ferry was approached by ancient packhorse routes. On the west side, the route was to Kilmichael Glassary, and on the Cowal side to Glendaruel, and on to the head of the Holy Loch.

In 1770, the ferry charges were 6d for a single man, 3d each for parties of

ten or more, and 9d for a man and a horse. In 1790, the landowners petitioned
the Argyll Road Trustees to be allowed to close the ferry because it was nearly
deserted owing to the new road being carried forward on both sides of Loch
Fyne. The petition was granted, and the ferry was never reopened.

Colonel Gladwin thinks the Brainport ferry was probably a heavily-built
wooden boat of 20–25 ft in length, propelled by a single large sail when the
wind was convenient, and at other times by a pair of 10-ft sweeps. The dry
stone 'long house' structure of the eighteenth-century ferry house remains. It
must have been abandoned before the cholera epidemic of 1832, as had it been
occupied at that time, it would probably have been burnt like all the other
houses then in Brainport.

Otter

Otter ferry used to run across the entrance to upper Loch Fyne, spanning
the 1½ miles between the pier in Otter Bay on the east side of the loch (on
the road between Strachur and Kilfinan) and West Otter quay on the loch's
western shore (north of Glas Eilean and east of Port Ann, on the verge of
Asknish Forest, formerly part of Silvercraigs Estate). The mile-long Oitir
('sand or shingle bank') Spit is just south of the crossing, and the beacon at its
western end marks the narrow entrance to the upper loch.

In 1561, Robert Lamont of Silvercraigs notes in the list of his properties that,
with the property of Silvercraigs, there was the ferry to Otter: 'precious in
peace and war as a means of access'. A little later, in 1600, Pont the mapmaker
showed the crossing of 'Loch Fynn' from 'Kerry of Cowal' (Ardlamont) to
'the north end of the Carricks, Lochgilp' (Silvercraigs).

Such eighteenth-century records that I have found present a far from happy
state of affairs. The 1741 Synod of Argyll papers refer to Robert Fullerton of
Kilmartin and Archibald Lambie of Glassary going to interview a minister at
Kingarth on Bute. They put up smoke signals at West Otter ferry, but no boat
was available to get them across. They had to forgo their mission because they
could not get to Bute in time.

According to the *Provisions of the Commissioners of Supply for Argyll*, Mr
Douglas was appointed in 1744 to finish the work at the quay at East Otter,
inhabitants between the waters of Evan and Drum, with their horses, being
expected to assist for two days. In 1747, it was noted that several years earlier,
£10 of the bridge money had been allocated to building a quay at West Otter
and paid to Dugald MacTavish of Dunarddary, but that it had not yet been
built. The aforesaid sum was to be paid by Dunarddary to Provost James
Fisher of Inveraray, and by him 'applied in the manner above mentioned'.
As many inhabitants of Kilfinan 'as the overseer shall judge proper' were
to work three days on the quay at East Otter. In 1748, John Campbell of

Otter reported to a meeting that the quay at East Otter had not yet been completed, and that 'what is already done thereto will be lost unless some more money is laid out to finish it'. On the same occasion, Provost Fisher of Inveraray complained that Dunarddary had not yet paid to him the £10 of bridge money that was put in his hands for repairing the quay at East Otter. The meeting appointed Dunarddary the Younger to lay out the aforesaid sum, 'otherwise that the Collector pursues him'.

Thirteen years later, in 1761, James Campbell, a merchant of Inveraray, complained that West Otter ferry had no quay or landing place, 'which renders boating of horses there almost impracticable'. There was no other way of getting horses on board than by making them jump off a slanting rock into the boat. In consequence, £12 of public funds was to be used for building a quay with the labour of the inhabitants of Silvercraigs. In 1762, James Campbell of Silvercraigs petitioned for funds to make a quay at West Otter ferry. William Douglas, a mason, had given him advice on the most appropriate method of carrying out the work. He was granted £12 to finish the quay and render it 'tolerably commodious'. In 1769, there was a complaint of bad service at Otter Ferry.

In his *Highland Tours in 1802 to 1804,* James Hogg tells of his encounter with Otter ferry:

At Ochter we were obliged to tarry some time, for although the wind was perfectly fair for our passage being southeasterly, yet the skipper refused to venture out. Being ushered into a room we asked for strong ale, which the house at first denied, but seeing that we did not call for anything else, a boy at last came into the room and creeping into a hole in the wall out of sight, pulled out two or three bottles of it by the neck. I observed to him that that was the smugglers' hole, which he positively denied.

Our ferrymen were at last persuaded to set out, but not until we were obliged to promise them sixpence for each passenger, which were now seven, over and above the common freight. This they charged on pretence that they could not get back that night and that they would be obliged to pay for their lodgings. Yet mark the rogue, they were home before we got out of their sight. Amongst our fellow passengers were two country girls, of the better order, from Lorn. The day being very rough, we run down to the dock and seeing the boat half filled with vernal birks, and not doubting but it was the same in which we should pass, I stepped into it, laid me down on the bieldy [lee] side, desiring the prettiest of the girls to take up her berth in my bosom. She complied without hesitation and I screened her with my mantle. Oh how my companions envied my situation!

When the sailors came how great was my mortification to find we have all taken up our stations in the wrong boat. We were all obliged to shift, and I being farthest in, was last in getting out, and lost not only my dearest bosom friend but every tolerable seat in the boat, being forced to sit grinning with my face in the weather all the way!

The 1891 *Schedule of Particulars as to Ferries* records the ferry at Otter as being a large boat, carrying about fifteen passengers, and used both for ferrying passengers to the steamer and across the loch. The ferryman was officially bound to carry cattle, but there were 'no fixed rules about this'. The fare was 1s 6d in daytime, and double that before sunrise and after sunset. In the end, it was noted that 'the ferry is hardly ever used as there is daily communication by steamer six days a week in spring, summer and autumn and four days a week in the winter'.

In spite of steamer competition, the ferry was still functioning eighteen years later, according to the 1909 *Return of Ferries*. The fare was still 1s 6d per person, but reduced to 1s when paying for more than two passengers. The ferry was run from East Otter and carried passengers only. The pier at West Otter was maintained by the District Ferry Committee.

The ferry survived at least until the outbreak of the Second World War. Roni Cameron, for many years in charge of the Argyll County Council road and ferry workshops, remembered one of his men, John Dunlop, crossing by Otter ferry with his bicycle at least once a week in the 1930s, in pursuit of his courtship at Tighnabruaich. With the expansion of motor transport after the war, most ferries, in order to remain viable, had to become capable of carrying vehicles. The 1948 Ministry of Transport Committee on Ferries effectively pronounced the death sentence on the Otter ferry when it recommended no vehicular ferry for the Port of Ann–Otter Ferry crossing. Strangely enough, references to the Otter ferry persisted in the *West Coast Of Scotland Pilot* well into the 1970s.

Portavadie–Tarbert

Portavadie to Tarbert was an old ferry route across the mouth of Loch Fyne, from Ardlamont to Knapdale. The ferry originally ran from Ascog on the Ardlamont side about one mile south of Portavadie. That landing became silted up, and the ferry moved to Portavadie, but it left its name to Ascog Loch and Ascog Castle (see Glossary). *Lamonts Clan History*, by Sheriff Hector Mackechnie, gives the old ferry from Portavadie the spelling 'Port-a-Mhadaidh' ('Port of the Fox'). I have been told by another authority that this derivation is wrong, and that the correct one is 'Port-a-Bhata' ('Port of the Boat').

In my time, the ferry was first revived for a relatively short period in the 1970s, when a giant dock was being dug at Portavadie for building oil rigs, and workmen had to be brought across from Tarbert. The venture left behind a big hole in the ground at Portavadie. The craft used for that service was a hydrofoil with its foils cut off. The most recent revival happened in July 1994, when Caledonian MacBrayne started running a successful summer service with a 'Scottish Island' type of vehicular ferry for six cars. At the time of writing a biger *Loch* does ferry runs all year round and crosses twelve times a day in high summer.

Inveraray to St Catherines

The origin of this ferry goes back to the Middle Ages, but all that I could discover about that era is that the ferry was then free for priests, blind people and pilgrims.

In 1680, John MacCurry, 'the ferrier', was in trouble: the magistrates of Inveraray ordained that he was 'either to find caution to maintain the new ferry boat or to demit his charge'. The boat had just been bought from Greenock for 50 merks. In 1695, Archibald the earl of Argyll granted 'the two merkland of Kilcatrine' to James Campbell on condition that 'he will ferry us and all our domestik servants . . . horses and goods, without payment . . . as in time begone and in all time coming'.

From the beginning of the eighteenth century, the ferry, the ferry boat and the ferry house in the old town of Inveraray were being put up to public roup (auction) by the burgh magistrates. When the then 'ferrier', Archibald McNokard, died in 1720, the 'sett and lett of the common ferrie' passed to one John Campbell, subject to his giving half of the profits to Margaret McNokard, 'relict of the deceist ferrier', together with the north end of the ferry house and half of the yard during the magistrates' pleasure. The same John Campbell, 'Maltman of Inveraray', won the roup in 1721 and was awarded a three-year contract. At the end of it, he became liable for penalty of £40 for not fulfilling the contract, and he was expected to leave behind a randle tree, for which his successor was to pay £3 14s. (A randle tree was a bar set into a chimney for hanging pots.)

In 1724, the magistrates succeeded in raising the rent of the ferry and ferry house to £24 16s Scots, and with the £12 left over from the previous year's house rent, they managed to cover the £36 spent on repairing the ferry boat. In 1742, the ferry and house were let jointly for seven years to William McGibbon, customs officer, and Donald McNicol. However, McGibbon could have the whole house and garden to himself if he paid McNicol £12 per year. On the other hand, His Grace the Duke could at any time demolish the house and garden, in which event 'the tack shall become null and void as concerns the said house and garden'.

In the new town, built in the middle of the eighteenth century, Inveraray's Ferryland contained the ferryman's house, in part of which he kept the ferry inn or dram shop to supplement his income. The ferry inn lasted till 1917, but at the time of writing part of Ferryland is still inhabited by the last ferryman's widow.

Moses Griffith's view of Inverary Castle, 1771 (loaned by Mrs Sheila MacIntyre)

There do not seem to have been any ferry piers at Inveraray or St Catherines until the mid-eighteenth century. In 1759, the Commissioners of Supply for Argyll allowed £100 towards building a pier at Inveraray, the inhabitants having to perform the work. In 1760, the inhabitants were again required to work at the pier. Duncan Stewart, a Chelsea pensioner, was fined 9s for not performing statute work. In 1764, Donald Campbell of St Catherines asked for assistance in building 'a key and breastwork' at St Catherines and a sum of £24 14s was allowed by the commissioners.

The dawn of fast travel by sea which came with the *Comet* in 1812 brought steamers to Loch Fyne. By 1820, three steamers were serving Inveraray, according to *Lumsden's Steamboat Companion* of that year: the *Argyll*, commissioned in 1815, the *Neptune* and the *Inveraray Castle,* of 1816 and 1819 respectively. In addition, a new road cut through Hell's Glen between St Catherines and Lochgoilhead at that time meant that a coach meeting Clyde steamer passengers at Lochgoilhead could drive them over the pass to the ferry at St Catherines.

In 1827, a David Napier proposed to run a small steamer, *Thalia,* between Strachur and Inveraray, and he asked the Inveraray Burgh Council what dues would be expected of him. The council was interested, and advised him to offer a lump sum for the year and to make an allowance for the loss of income by the existing town's ferry. David, whose uncle, Robert, was the blacksmith to the duke, applied to be enrolled as a burgess freeman, which would exempt

Sketch by author of the Ferry Inn, Inverary (Ferryland)

him from all dues. In that year, he had two steamers on the ferry route, the *Thalia* and the *Robert Bruce*. In 1828, Robert himself became the lessee of the ferry at an annual rent of £51. The following year, however, the Loch Goil and Loch Long Steamboat Company, of which the duke was a shareholder, obtained a lease of the ferry which lasted until 1865.

The company ran a steamer from Inveraray to St Catherines twice a day in the summer and once a day in the winter. From 1856, the *Argyll*, built by Wingate and Company, was that steam ferry. The ferry had a coach connection from St Catherines to Lochgoilhead, and Black's *Picturesque Tourist of Scotland*, published in the 1850s, describes that connection through Hell's Glen:

> A four-horse coach runs regularly from the Lochgoilhead steamer to St. Catherine pier opposite Inveraray. The distance is seven miles and the road so steep that a good pedestrian may, without great exertion, arrive at St. Catherine before the coach. At St. Catherine a steamer awaits passengers and conveys them across the Loch to Inveraray. Cabin fare is one shilling and steerage sixpence.

In mid-Victorian times, the coachman who drove through Hell's Glen to St Catherines was also St Catherines' inn-keeper. He was a renowned local character and raconteur who kept his customers amused with his tales of

Inverary from the south, by J.M.W. Turner, c. 1801 (loaned by Mrs Sheila MacIntyre)

rural doings and of his brushes with Lord Palmerston, poet Martin Tupper and Lord Tennyson, who was a friend of the 8th duke and visited him in 1857. An anonymous visitor from Dover in 1856 describes the coachman, John Campbell, as: 'a man of extraordinary natural abilities. He kept a roar of laughter by relating anecdotes told with the most inimitable humour.' At the end of such a journey, who would not contribute to the funds he was raising to build a school at St Catherines? He raised £150, and in 1857, Pole School was founded with Masonic Honours.

Unfortunately the steam ferry service did not pay. The rent was reduced to £35, which the company refused to pay in 1864, offering £20, but eventually settling for £30. In the mean time, there were complaints that the steamer was not powerful enough for bad-weather service. In 1864, a group of Inveraray citizens, including the duke of Argyll, formed the new Inveraray Ferry and Coach Company. They outbid the Loch Goil Company with a bid for £48. Their ferry was to be a little paddlesteamer, the *Fairy*, built in 1865 at Port Glasgow, 60 ft long, 13 ft in beam, of 25 gross tons and powered by a 15 h.p. steam engine. To start with, the *Fairy* ran between Inveraray and Strachur, from which the company's two-horse coach carried passengers to Dunoon pier. In response, the Lochgoil people sent their steamer to Strachur and their coach to Kilmun pier on the Holy Loch. The Inveraray company then switched their ferry to St Catherines, to connect with the Lochgoilhead

The Steamer **FAIRY** can be had

FOR **HIRE** AS UNDER:—

ARDKINGLAS, when not exceeding Twelve Passengers,			12/6
STRACHUR,	„	„ „	13/6
FURNACE,	„	Eighteen „	18/
CRARAE,	„	Twenty „	20/
MINARD,	„	„ „	25/
ARDRISHAIG,	„	„ „	50/

GOODS AS PER AGREEMENT.

When Steamer is detained at any place it may be hired to a charge at the rate of 4s. an hour will be made.

FERRY RATES BY STEAMER BETWEEN INVERARAY & ST. CATHERINES.

ONE SHILLING is the fare in fore or after part of Steamer.

RETURN FARES, at ONE SHILLING, are issued for crossing and returning with Steamer same day.

SIXPENCE is charged for crossing and returning with same run of Steamer.

BY ROWING OR SAILING BOATS.

From Six a.m. to Nine p.m. the fare is ONE SHILLING for a single passenger, and SIXPENCE each when more than one.

From Nine p.m. to Six a.m. the fares are double.

The Steamer can be had to St. Catherines at other than the advertised hours at the ordinary ferry rates, with a minimum charge of 5s. when the steam is up, and 7s. 6d. when steam is raised specially.

RATES FOR HORSES, CATTLE, etc.

Horses, 1/3 each; Cattle, 1/; Sheep, 1/6 score. Carriages—2-wheeled, 2/6; 4-wheeled, 4/. Hay and Straw, 6d. a bale; Meal, Flour, Oats, Wool, etc, 6d. a bag. Beer, Oil, Grease, etc., 6d. a barrel.

Other Goods according to Weight or Bulk.

J. RODGER, Manager.

INVERARAY STEAM FERRY CO., Limited,
APRIL, 1887.

Advertisement for the *Fairy*, April 1887 (loaned by the Argyll Archivist) coach. *The Tourist Guide Book* of the 1870s refers to a 'large well-appointed coach serving St. Catherine whence the steamer "Fairy" sails for Inveraray'.

Competition between the two ferry companies produced a curious situation. The *Argyll* continued to operate on behalf of the Loch Goil Company but discontinued paying fees to Inveraray. The *Fairy* did not renege on its fees, and it charged a reduced fare to passengers using their own coach to travel to Lochgoilhead. Each company paid the 'ferrier' representing the 1695 appointment by the then earl of Argyll 6d 5d and later 3d as compensation for every passenger carried by the steamer. The steamer fare at that time was 1s per passenger, and the sailing boat fare 6d. Inveraray Town Council raised an action for the arrestment of the *Argyll*, and in response, the Loch Goil Company petitioned for ferry regulations to be laid down. In 1867, the Inveraray District Road Trustees did draw up regulations for the ferry, one of which was that the ferry must sail at fixed times, irrespective of whether she had passengers.

In the late 1860s, some 4,000 passengers were conveyed annually by the *Fairy*, bringing a gross income of around £200. This would seem a good return on the original capital outlay of £1,100. However, the expenses could not have been negligible, because the Inveraray company paid no dividends, even after the *Argyll* disappeared, leaving the *Fairy* to paddle across on her own. The traffic must have been steadily declining, because by 1881, the Lochgoilhead coach was withdrawn and the annual ferry rent fell to £31.

In 1892, the ferry company's manager, John Rodger, who also happened to be the Inveraray apothecary, applied for the ferry to be exempt from having to hold a Board of Trade certificate, because the 'Company is unable to expend the necessary amount'. To augment the *Fairy*'s receipts, she was made available for hire and could be had for a cruise to Ardrishaig with up to twenty passengers for 50s. She was hired by the Inveraray Town Council to carry councillors and their wives on a celebratory cruise on Loch Fyne when Inveraray's first wooden pier was completed. Her publicity was boosted by a ballad, 'Fairy in the Fog', to the tune of 'Kitty of Lochgoil', bewailing the ferry being lost in the fog on her passage across Loch Fyne.

The Fairy in the Fog

'Twas in the year of eighty one
On Januar the fourth day
The steamer Fairy crossed Loch Fyne
For sweet St Catherine's bay.

Our captain bold was Duncan Bell
The pilot Donuil Dubh
The engineer Shon Gillies
And Dugal Piobair was the crew.

The day with fog was thick and dark;
You could neither hear nor see
But Donuil Dubh just kept her nose
Straight for St Catherine's Quay.

The passengers were soon on board
That Coachie Hugh had brought
And then again through blinding fog
Our homeward way we sought.

In coming back the dreadful fog
Got thicker than before.
Said Captain Bell to Donuil Dubh,
'We'll creep along the shore.'

The pilot at his stemmy post
Stood firm as any rock,
With the compass true before his eyes
Just like my Grandfather's clock.

As we came near the Newtown Bay
Tho' our reckoning scarce could fail
Said Dugal Piobair to himself
'I wish we saw the jail.'

The Captain kept a sharp look out
And in case of need
He told his trusty engineer
To slacken off her speed

As he went cautiously along
Prepared to heave the lead
The first thing that we noticed
Was a small buoy right ahead.

The Captain he stood on the deck
A few feet from the funnel
And to the Pilot passed a word,
'Keep clear of Mackenzie's Tunnel.'

Already we were shearing off
Our course we knew quite well
When through the fog some lengths away
There came a dismal yell.

'Now what was that?' the Captain cried
'I ne'er hear the like before.'
Said Dugal Piobair,
'Sure it was A Pochkan on the shore.'

Sketch by the author of St Catherines pier

In spite of all these activities, the Inveraray company decided to give up ferrying, and the town council had to take over the ferry as a municipal enterprise in 1892. The 1891 Schedule of Argyll Ferries refers to two rowing or sailing ferries between Inveraray and St Catherines, one of 19-ft keel carrying ten passengers and the other of 14-ft keel, also carrying ten passengers. It quotes a fare of 4s for a four-wheeled carriage, 2s 6d for a two-wheeled carriage, 1s for a single passenger and 6d each when more than one were carried; between 9 p.m. and 6 a.m. the fares were doubled.

A steamer, yet another *Fairy*, was built to the order of the town council at Blackhilll Dock in Glasgow at a cost of £1,350, of which £700 was lent by the 'Duachnach Lodge of Ancient Shepherds'. She was fitted with diagonal compound engines and achieved a speed of 9½ miles per hour at her second trial. Her captain was to receive an annual salary of £60, her manager £10 per year, and an Inveraray lad appointed as her deckhand was to receive 13s per week.

The year 1907 produced a record profit of £250 for the ferry, but in 1908 the repairs requested by the Board of Trade surveyor caused the steamer ferry to be sold at Greenock for £70. The ferry was let to John Dewar, an Inveraray gentleman who undertook to keep a steam or motor vessel certificated by the Board of Trade for thirty-four persons, a large boat for beasts, and in addition, a small yawl for passengers. He had the *Fairy* overhauled and brought back from Greenock. In the five years John Dewar was ferryman, he had to contend with a number of calamities, ranging from a pirate ferry operator to a great gale which swept the west coast in November 1912, drove the *Fairy*

Hope MacArthur (loaned by Mrs Jean MacArthur)

ashore and wrecked her at the Salmon Draught. This brought about John Dewar's resignation and ended the steamer era in Inveraray.

Towards the end of 1913, a new ferryman, Duncan Bell, plied the loch with his steam launch *Kate*, enjoying an annual subsidy of £50. *Kate* was described as narrow and wobbly, and on one stormy crossing, the passenger and skipper had to lash themselves to the mast, 'just in case'.

James Douglas, 'a first rate seaman', ran the ferry from 1919 to 1937 with his own 30-ft long Loch Fyne skiff, *Dolphin*, into which he installed an engine. In addition to the subsidy, he was allowed the use of the ferry house at the nominal rent of £7 per year. In 1920 he was granted a fare increase for the first time since 1887. The motorboat fare to St Catherines became 5s for up to four passengers, and 1s 6d for each additional passenger, 1½ fare being charged at night and on Sundays. The rowing boat or sailing skiff fare became 3s for up to four passengers and 1s for each additional one. Horses were to be charged at 3s each, and a 'baby coach', bicycle or beer barrel 1s 6d. A day return was 1s 6d, but crossing and returning on the same run cost 1s. In the 1930s, a bus service was started between St Catherines and Dunoon by Macdonald of the St Catherines Hotel.

John 'Doda' MacArthur ferried with his motorboat *Happy Return,* with a significantly increased subsidy, from 1937 to 1942, when he went to fight in the war. There was a successor, and then a lapse before Hope MacArthur, John's brother, and at one time James Douglas's crewmate, took over. In addition to his brother's *Happy Return,* Hope had the *Jean* built by Weatherhead's at Eyemouth. In his time, the subsidy rose to £130 from the town and £70 from the county.

Hope had four regular runs from Inveraray, at 8. 15 a.m., 11 a.m., 2.30 p.m. and 6.30 p.m. A day return on each of them was 2s 6d, and a special run was charged at 8s. This timetable was intended to fit in with the times of Montgomery's bus from Dunoon and MacConnachie's from Campbeltown, in conjunction with which the service offered a short cut on the Campbeltown–Glasgow route by cutting out the then very slow 'Rest and be Thankful' road. Hope used to put up a white flag at the pier when he had passengers for the Campbeltown-bound bus. Passengers boarding his 8.15 a.m. ferry for St Catherines could get to Glasgow before 11 a.m. via the Dunoon bus, the Dunoon–Gourock ferry and the train from Gourock to Glasgow.

Hope was a 'character' and a wit. At least one of his ferry boats was capable of carrying over thirty passengers and was liable for an annual Board of Trade Survey. One winter's day, I was on my way to Inveraray pier and the ferry boat, and as I approached the town, I was confronted by the lowest part of the lochside road being under water because of an unusually high flood tide and a south-westerly gale. I attempted to brave through, but my Morris Traveller stalled in the flood, and I had to wait for the tide to turn. All the time, Hope was on the pier, peering through his binoculars at the unhappy Board of Trade Traveller, its picture in colour being well engraved in the communal memory of Argyll's marine fraternity When I at last materialised at the pier, he greeted me with: 'Mister Surveyor, its your car that needs loadline marking more than my boat!'

Hope tried to augment the ferry's income with 'half-a-crown' (2s 6d) cruises down the loch to Minard Castle, where he could also sometimes pick up holidaymakers wanting a trip to Inveraray. In 1963, however, he decided to swap the ferryman's job for that of school janitor. His successor carried on for only another year, when the county withdrew its subsidy and the ferry service came to an end.

INVERARAY - St. CATHERINES

FERRY SERVICE

DAILY (EXCEPT SUNDAYS)

Leave Inveraray	Leave St. Catherines
AT	AT APPROXIMATELY
8.15 a.m.	8.30 a.m.
(Connection to Glasgow via Dunoon)	
11.00 a.m.	11.20 a.m.
	Connection from Glasgow via Dunoon (Leave Glasgow Central at 8.29 a.m.)
2.30 p.m.	2.50 p.m.
(Connection to Glasgow via Dunoon)	
6.30 p.m. (except Saturdays)	6.50 p.m.
	Connection from Glasgow Via Dunoon (Leave Glasgow Central at 3.55)
7.30 p.m. (Sat. only)	8.15 p.m.
	Connection from Glasgow Via Dunoon (Leave Glasgow Central 5.20 p.m.)

FARES and CHARGES

Ordinary single fare	- 2s. per passenger
Ordinary return fare, same run	- 2s. per passenger
„ same day	- 2s. 6d. per passenger
Special Ferry, 1 to 3 persons	- 6s.
„ over 3 persons	- Ordinary fares

SPECIAL FERRY can be had at any time (including Sundays)
MOTOR LAUNCH CRUISES daily from Pier.   Special parties catered for.

HOPE McARTHUR, Ferryman.

Advertisement for the Inverary to St Catherines ferry, 1950s (loaned by Mrs Jean MacArthur)

13

MORVERN TO MOIDART

From Morvern in the south to Moidart in the north, and from Ardgour in the east to Ardnamurchan in the west, stretches a large, mountainous peninsula, bounded on the east by the wide sweep of Loch Linnhe and on the south the Sound of Mull. The peninsula is divided into four by Loch Sunart, running roughly east-west, and Loch Shiel, running north-east to south-west. Before the days of the motor car, travel between these four areas and to the world beyond was easier by boat than having to circumvent lochs by road. From the earliest times, Loch Sunart carried most of the traffic between Morvern and Ardnamurchan and a good deal of the traffic between Morvern and Ardgour.

Loch Sunart

In 1749, Alexander MacLachlan of 'Ligisdale' (Liddesdale), an area of lead mines, petitioned the Commission of Supply for Argyll, 'Craving they would grant their warrant and authority for establishing a ferry at Ligisdale to transport passengers from thence to the opposite shore . . . to Ellanvourich' (Eilean a 'Mhuirich, one mile west of Strontian on the north side of the loch). The commission recommended that Donald Campbell of Airds consider the usefulness of such a ferry, what freights might be exacted from passengers and make a report to the next general meeting.

There is little information in the form of drawings about the boats that plied on Loch Sunart and other lochs of the region in the mid-eighteenth century. However, from contemporary illustrated maps, carvings and even literary descriptions, it may be surmised that they were probably double-ended, square-sailed and that their hulls were punctured with oar-ports suitable for flat-handled oars, perhaps with a long slot to the left of each port to allow the oar blade to pass through from within the ship. (These oar-ports were retained in later designs because they were convenient for carrying boats.)

The Liddesdale ferry was still active in the first half of the twentieth century. A small boat rowed by the Laudale Estate workers used to go

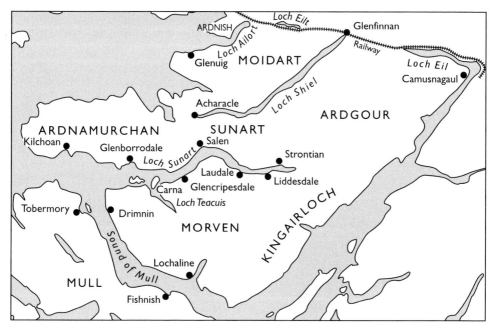

Morvern, Moidart, Ardgour and Ardnamurchan

across to Camuschoirk, on the main road between Strontian and Salen. It was run mainly for the benefit of Laudale Estate workers and lead miners working at Achagavel (a couple of miles south of Liddesdale, off the main Lochaline road).

Further west, about half-way along Loch Sunart, another rowing ferry of moderate size used to ply between the mouth of Glencripesdale Burn on the Morvern (southern) shore and Camasinas on the Ardnamurchan (northern) side of the loch, on the shore road from Glenborrodale to Salen. The ferry boat was run by Alan MacDougal of Glencripesdale until his death in 1929, when Sam Cameron took over and ferried until the Second World War. Every weekday at 4 p.m., Royal Mail would be conveyed to and from Glencripesdale jetty. The mail would then be carried the six or so miles on the road from Camasinas to Acharacle, at first by horse and cart, and later by bus. From Acharacle, there was a regular steamer service the length of Loch Shiel to Glenfinnan, the LNER railhead on the Glasgow–Mallaig line. Other than at mail times, the ferry could be summoned from Glencripesdale in daylight by a smoke signal set off on the rocks at Camasinas.

Alan MacDougal's niece, Mrs Macleod of Achleek, near Liddesdale, told me of her young days between the wars in Glencripesdale. She said that apart from her uncle's ferry and the route via Acharacle, there were two other, even more tortuous, ways of reaching the bright city lights from the southern shore of Loch Sunart. One could walk along the footpath from Glencripesdale to Kinlochteacuis and try to borrow a bicycle there. If successful, one could cycle to Lochaline and embark on the MacBrayne's mail steamer *Lochinvar* for Oban. The other way was to take the loch-shore track to Liddesdale and the road from Lochaline to Strontian and onwards, through Glen Tarbert and along the Ardgour shore, either to Corran ferry, to cross to Onich and Ballachulish railway station, or to Camusnagaul ferry, to cross to Fort William. It used to take a good half day to walk the fifteen miles from Liddesdale to Corran, and most of a day to walk to Camusnagaul.

The ferry at the mouth of Loch Sunart – from Glenborrodale on the Ardnamurchan side, crossing the narrows between the islands of Risga and Carna to Doirlinn, behind Carna on the Morvern side – was noted in about 1800 as the only regular ferry across the loch. There was then a changehouse at Doirlinn, which would support the notion that the ferry ran regularly. A track leads to Doirlinn from Drimnin, and there was also a track along the west shore of Loch Teacuis to Kinlochteacuis and on to Kinlochaline, which no longer exists. As recently as between the wars, boats from Glenborrodale provided an occasional ferry service on the crossing. The route was particularly in demand to ferry funerals from Ardnamurchan to the Camerons' burial ground at Mungosdail, near Drimnin, where there is also an early Celtic church.

Two 50 ft wooden sailing smacks of about 30 ton deadweight, the *Mary* and *Effie,* carried supplies across and up and down the Sound of Mull and Loch Sunart in the first quarter of this century. They had no engines, but boasted giant steering wheels on the open flush decks. Each boat had a single mast, with a boom carrying the mainsail which also served to discharge cargo with the help of a small 1 cwt windlass of wooden construction. At each pier, the boom and the windlass were operated by the customers themselves, who took away their purchases of coal and other bulk supplies in horse-drawn carts. The owner/skipper was John Neil MacPhee, a big, bearded man. A smaller, bearded man used to pull the oars in a little boat which acted as the smack's tug in the vicinity of rocks and harbour approaches. He always seemed to be around when MacPhee needed him, otherwise, he was reputed to disappear into one of the Gallanach caves, near Oban.

The smack could manoeuvre under sail in Loch Sunart, but when it came to making her way behind Carna Island into Loch Teacuis, MacPhee had to fall back on his knowledge of local currents and the boat/tug which pulled him with a towline perhaps 200 ft long. The little oarsman would rest on his square-bladed oars for a while, and then, in response to the skipper's shout, he would spring into action to help steer the smack. The 'tugmaster' would then rest on his oars again until another frantic pull was required, into the narrows of Loch Teacuis. The smack would be beached on the loch's shore and her contents unloaded. A little steamer, the *Brenda,* was more or less contemporary with the *Mary* and the *Effie,* and she also used to ferry goods up and down Loch Sunart, her final destination being Tobermory.

The car and the lorry have replaced the ferries in the last half-century, since they can travel the length of the north shore of Loch Sunart and not only reach Lochaline but even Drimnin and Rahoy on Loch Teacuis. All internal ferry services of this region have disappeared, although no more of the south shore of Loch Sunart is accessible by road today than was the case in the mid-eighteenth century, when 'the Commissioners of Supply for Argyll decreed that half the inhabitants of Sunart are to work on making a road from the head of Loch Sunart to Liddesdale'. Depopulation was probably as responsible as the advent of motor transport in making the Doirlinn, Liddesdale and Glencripesdale ferries uneconomical.

Loch Aline

The ferry across the mouth of Loch Aline, known as the Caolas ferry, was intended to save the long trek from Ardtornish Bay to Lochaline via Claggan bridge, before one was built across the River Aline at Kinlochaline. Although it is likely that there was an earlier one, the extant ferry pier at Lochaline was

Island class *Rhum* at Loch Aline in 1992

begun in 1847 under the supervision of the minister, John Macleod, and was completed by the Fishery Board in the following year. It provided work for thirty-one families who were receiving aid during the potato famine. Before a public road-building programme got under way, a private road was built in the 1850s, on the east side of Loch Aline, to link Achranich township at the head of the loch with the Caolas ferry 2½ miles away.

Latterly, the ferry ran mainly to take children from Ardtornish and Achranich to school in Lochaline village. The service ceased on the departure of the last ferryman, Mr Ives, who was employed by the Ardtornish Estate. Anyway, I doubt if today's children would be enthusiastic about a daily walk of three miles to the ferry. The pier is still in fairly good order, and until recently, one still could find there the old bell which was used for summoning the ferryman from his abode on the Ardtornish side. The Lochaline ferry pier has rarely been used by ships, because water swirls past it at 5 knots at half-tide, and because it is too shallow at low water.

Lochailort

At the northern end of Moidart, a ferry survived longer than the Loch Sunart ferries. Lochailort, a natural haven at the head of the Sound of Arisaig, which saw the landing and re-embarkation of Prince Charles Edward Stewart, and in 1746 the last battle of the Jacobite Rebellion, used to be the railhead terminal for the Glenuig ferry further west, which remained in service until the construction of the Lochailort-Acharacle road in the 1960s. The ferry was unique because, rather than bridging a water barrier, it connected two jetties on the coast of Moidart.

I visited the ferry for a survey in June 1958 and was carried the length of its route, some seven miles. We sailed down Loch Ailort, with Sean Cruachan towering to port at first and then the rocky shore of the Ardnish peninsula to starboard and the massif of An Stoc and Rois Bheinn on the other side. The ferryman pointed out to me the solitary house on the peninsula at Laggan – apparently, it had no phone and was inhabited by a Harris man, Donald Macleod, who retired there from Patagonia. Through the narrows between the Bairneach and Gualainn islands, we emerged into the open Sound of Arisaig and Glenuig Bay. In those days, Glenuig was a very isolated township – one could not make a local call from the one and only telephone in the village, because the nearest telephones were at Lochailort to the north and Acharacle to the south, outside the 'local' zone.

The skipper/owner of the ferry was 'Whaler' Macdonald, who got the nickname when he returned home from working in South Georgia in the 1930s. The route on which he ran his two ferry boats in summer and winter could be a dangerous one and required an experienced and accomplished

'Whaler' Macdonald with the author on the Lochailort–Glenuig ferry in 1958

sailor like him. There were days when westerly gales funnelled into the loch and waterspouts could occur. On one stormy night, the ferry's rudder sheared off, and Whaler had to drive the boat ashore at Laggan.

The ferry carried passengers, mail, baggage and every kind of merchandise to and from Glenuig three days a week, but Thursday was 'rations' day, when the weekly supply of victuals was picked up off the train from Fort William. At the time of my 1958 visit, one of the ferries was an ex-ships lifeboat, built by Maclean's of Renfrew, called *Am Eala*. The other was an ex-lobster fishing boat, built by Weatherhead's of Cockenzie and called *Guide Me*.

Mr Macdonald very hospitably invited me to take tea at his Glenuig home. There I met his wife and their very young family – all Gaelic speakers, and none of the children had, as yet, a word of English.

I understand that a bigger boat, the 36-ft *Jacobite,* with a wooden double-diagonal hull and a Lister diesel engine, was brought from Bowling on the Clyde in 1960. She served as a ferry until 1968, when the new road was opened and ferrying ceased.

While the Glenuig ferry was replaced by a road and the other 'internal' ferries of the region withered away, the four which for centuries have been its gateways to and from the world outside have survived to this day. One plies across each end of the Sound of Mull, as described later, and the other two span the top stretch of Loch Linnhe.

Loch Linnhe

The ferry across the Corran Narrows on Loch Linnhe, between Ardgour and Onich, has been significant since the Middle Ages. It is recorded that in the fifteenth century, it came into the possession of the Macleans of Duart. In the eighteenth century, it was the nearest point in the region to the military road running along the far side of Loch Linnhe. In 1745, the ferry came to a temporary halt when soldiers devastated the village of Ardgour, a little to the west of Corran. Around 1800, a 'parliamentary' road was built from Corran ferry to the head of Loch Sunart and on to Kinlochmoidart.

Apart from its strategic value, the ferry was part of a drove route. Cattle from Strontian Market were driven through Glen Tarbert and along the Ardgour shore to Corran, where they sometimes had to swim the 'Lochaber Current' to join a good drove route south and east via Ballachulish ferry and Glencoe. The Glen Tarbert route may not have been a major one, but none the less it is shown as a fairly good road on the Argyll farm plans of 1819.

The Corran ferry piers were built in 1817, and Thomas Telford was concerned with the building. The stone is understood to have been brought by sea from Strontian, having travelled the length of Loch Sunart, the Sound of Mull and most of Loch Linnhe. In the early part of the nineteenth century, the ferry started to carry mail, and in 1830, this six-day-week service earned it £17 6s per year.

Early in the period between the wars, the ownership of the ferry was taken over from the Macleans of Ardgour by Argyll County Council, the vessel being a 25-ft wooden boat propelled by a Kelvin petrol/paraffin engine. The ferry rights were then leased to Buchanan and MacIntosh, with John Buchanan as skipper. He was not a man to be rushed; as likely as not, one would have to look for him in the Corran hostelry and then one might have had to wait while he put fuel into the boat's tank. One one occasion, he went out without topping up the tank, nearly ran out of fuel, was carried away southwards by the tide and had to tie his boat to a buoy near Eilean Balnagowan, in Cuil Bay, off Appin. The passengers, including some schoolchildren, had to wait for the tide to turn before the boat could drift up the loch and to the other side.

Just before the Second World War, the ferry came under the management of the MacIntosh family of the Nether Lochaber Hotel. By this time, it was a 50-ft wooden-turntable craft capable of carrying four cars, probably the first purpose-built car ferry in Scotland. The ferryman was then a MacPhee, but in 1945 he went to run the Bonawe ferry across Loch Etive, and Peter MacQueen was appointed. He remained in charge until 1974, the ferry in the mean time having reverted to local authority control, this time the Highland Regional Council. In the 1960s, a nine-car ferry built by Noble's of Fraserburgh came

The vehicle ferry at Corran pier, 1930s (loaned by the Scottish Ethnological Society)

into service, and more recently, *Eilean Dhu,* the steel ferry from the Black Isle with a capacity of some twenty-eight cars, was introduced.

The Camusnagaul ferry plies from the north-eastern corner of Ardgour to Fort William across the head of Loch Linnhe, at its confluence with Loch Eil. It is a passenger-only service, like the one across the Sound of Mull from Kilchoan to Tobermory. The present vessel is the *Cailin an Aiseag,* a 35-ft, steel motorboat built on the Moray Firth in 1981. She is the first purpose-built craft for the service. Since the take-over by Highland Regional Council in the 1970s, at least three second-hand boats have been tried on the crossing, none of them being quite satisfactory.

14

MULL

From the earliest times the island of Mull exported cattle to the mainland but due to local politics the ferry trade remained precarious at least until 1609, when the Privy Council annulled the recurring prohibition of all trade with Mull and the Western Isles. More troubles lay ahead for the Mull ferries as the mainland lairds tried unlawfully to exact tolls from cattle landings.

In spite of those obstacles Mull remained throughout the eighteenth and early nineteenth centuries one of the principal sources of Argyll droving traffic, sending to the mainland not only its own but also cattle collected from the neighbouring islands of Coll and Tiree.

The Sound

By the end of the eighteenth century the crossing from Ardnacross on the Aros shore of Mull to Rhemore in Morven, across the narrowest part of the Sound of Mull, was one of the only two regular cattle ferrying services between Mull and the mainland.

The other regular ferry route was from Auchnacraig on the south-east shore of Mull, or Grass Point at the mouth of Loch Don, to Barr-nam-Boc on the north-west shore of Kerrera, and from Ardantrive at the north-east end of Kerrera to Dunollie just north of Oban, described at length in Chapter 8.

There was a kind of stone landing slip at Ardnacross but at Rhemore there was no pier, only a natural inlet and a 'changehouse'. Some time during the first half of the nineteenth century, the mouth of Lochaline became linked by ferry with the pier at Bailemeonach on Mull. From 1848 the service used the extant ferry pier on the west side of Loch Aline. The drovers preferred this to the other Mull–Morvern ferries, probably because of the cattle sale at Loch Aline, which used to be held prior to the sale at Salen on Mull, which in turn generated traffic in the opposite direction from Loch Aline to Bailemeonach; some of that traffic found its way south via the Kerrera ferry (see Chapter 8).

Until the advent of the Sound of Mull steamers in the second half of the nineteenth century, mail came to Lochaline only once a week. It travelled via Oban, Kerrera, Grass Point and Bailemeonach – over two islands and by three ferries.

Even in 1872, it was still difficult to get to Lochaline. The Astley sisters, visiting Ardtornish in that year, complained in their letters that steamers from Oban to Tobermory did not always call at Lochaline. Only the smallest steamers could comfortably use the pier at other than flood tide, although a large paddlesteamer called annually to pick up two or three thousand sheep. The scheduled steamers normally had to anchor off the mouth of the loch, relying on small ferries to carry passengers and freight ashore. It was only in 1883 that a steamer pier was built on the deep shore round the corner from the ferry pier, so ending ship-to-shore ferrying. For about eighty years after this, there was no direct ferry between Lochaline and Mull, the demand being met by the Sound steamers.

In between the war years the Sound steamer operated the ferry service between Oban and Loch Aline. On most days in the summer the *Lochinvar* left Oban at 1.15 p.m. arriving at Lochaline 1½ hours later. However since the connecting train arrived much earlier in the morning passengers who wanted to avoid a long wait could charter the *Princess Louise*, a handsome little craft of 106 tons, acquired by MacBrayne in 1934 to act as a relief for the *Lochinvar*.

Drimmin, on the Morvern shore of the Upper Sound, apart from being the destination of funeral processions, was in the early part of twentieth century, and even between the wars, a collecting point for mail, which was taken to MacBrayne cargo steamers by 20–30 ft shore-to-ship ferries. These used to have a short forecastle to protect the well, in which horses, cattle or sheep could be carried, as well as the mail. Engines were not installed in them until the late 1920s or early '30s. A boat with an engine could then, if need be, tow one or two other boats. Two jetties are at present still traceable near Drimnin, as well as a massive, disused pier at Fiunary between Drimnin and Lochaline.

In the late 1960s, vehicular ferries were introduced on the west coast, gradually replacing the scheduled steamer services. The original 'Island' class Caledonian MacBrayne ferry on the Fishnish–Lochaline crossing carried only eight small cars. The present large ferry, which plies in the summer and carries some thirty cars, started her life on the Cumbrae run in the Clyde. The winter ferry carries only twelve cars, but this is still more than the one she replaced. Their skipper at the time of writing is Callum McKechnie, whose father, Ian, was for years the Gigha ferryman. In spite of the frequency of her service, the ferry is mostly used by passing tourists and is of little benefit to the people of Lochaline, even for shopping expeditions on foot. The Fishnish terminal is twelve miles from Tobermory and about six miles from Craignure or Salen on Mull. No wonder they sigh for the old days of the *Lochinvar* and her successors, when they enjoyed a direct connection to Tobermory and Oban.

In the latter part of the nineteenth century, MacVicar's of Tobermory owned the *Anna Bhan*, a 50-ft smack, and worked her as a ferry between

Tobermory and Drimnin and places like Rhemore and Killundine, a little to the south in the Sound of Mull. More recently, between the wars, when the weather was too bad or the MacBrayne's steamer failed to call for any other reason, Camerons of Kilchoan used their sturdy shore-to-ship boat to provide an auxiliary mail ferry between Drimnin and Tobermory

Ardnamurchan to Tobermory

Between the wars, the same Cameron team – a father and two sons, who owned a store at Kilchoan in Ardnamurchan – connected Ardnamurchan with the outside world by running their rowing ferry to the Tobermory-bound Outer Islands steamer, *Plover,* and back to the Kilchoan shore, but sometimes, when necessary, even to Tobermory. At least one of the team was drowned in bad weather between Kilchoan and Tobermory.

Since the Second World War, *Loch Buie,* a fast ex-air-sea rescue wooden motor launch, was put on the Kilchoan–Tobermory ferry service by MacBrayne's. She was half-decked and had a square stern. Her skipper was Jackie Tague of Bunessan, in the Ross of Mull, brother-in-law to Captain Callum Robertson of the *Lochinvar.* Her engineer was a Tobermory gentleman, George Sproat, who was unfortunate enough to lose a finger in tending to the engine. It is said that he lost another finger demonstrating how the first accident happened. Today, a Loch class of Caledonian MacBayne vehicular ferry runs between Mingarry Castle near Kilchoan and Tobermory.

Oban to Mull

Once the cattle traffic between Mull and Oban via Kerrera declined with steamers taking over, the Oban to Mull ferrying was being done by the Sound steamer, which called at the Salen and Tobermory piers. The motor vessel *Lochinvar* – built in 1909 – spent all her long life, till well after the Second World War, on the Oban–Sound of Mull–Tobermory run. The vessel of fine lines and well designed hull was somewhat spoilt in appearance by an excessively short funnel and a crane which swung over the funnel. The crane allowed the *Lochinvar* to convey a few cars at a little inconvenience and not a little expense. She has lived long enough to become endeared to many people in Argyll for her consistently good service, and so did her captains Callum Black and Callum Robertson, and her purser John Mackenzie, Captain Robertson's son-in-law, who in time became a much respected Western Area Manager of Caledonian MacBrayne.

The *Lochinvar* was built as a triple engine and triple screw vessel. After the last war she was re-engined with two sets of Paxman motors turning twin screws, the single rudder remaining on the centre line, which somewhat

The *Lochinvar*

reduced her steering capabilities. After more than fifty years' faithful duty the *Lochinvar* was disposed of for scrap in the early 1960s. I was therefore beginning to disbelieve my eyes and to believe in ghost ships when one Saturday morning the *Lochinvar* made a slow entrance into James Watt loch in Greenock. Screwing my eyes somewhat I could decipher the name *Brighton Belle* in small letters on her bow. On that occasion I had to avail myself of my rarely used detention power to prevent a man and his young son from taking her to the south coast of England without any safety equipment. A few years later the *Lochinvar* was tragically lost with all on board her, having been driven onto the Donna Nook shore, south of the Humber, on her return voyage to Scotland. The impaired steering ability may have contributed to the loss of the ship.

At Craignure there was no pier until the car ferry came into operation in 1964, but for almost 200 years there was an inn which sheltered ferry passengers. Before the pier was built for the car ferry MacBrayne's steamers anchored in the bay and passengers had to descent through a side door into a ship-to-shore ferry boat moored alongside and disembark at the old stone slip. With the new linkspan ferry terminal the Oban–Craignure route has become the principal, the shortest and the most frequent ferry service between Mull and the mainland.

However, since the last war there has been for forty years a unique on-demand ferry service between Oban and Grass Point on Mull operated by Mrs Henrietta Spencer of Oban, for most of the time in association with her

The Craignure ferry

daughter Bella and son-in-law Donald McQueen. Her ferrying enterprise started with taking Sunday papers to Mull because MacBraynes did not provide a Sunday service. Summer and winter Muilichs read their papers on Sunday courtesy of the young Mrs Spencer, brought over in the *Island Queen*, a 36-ft ex-harbour launch from Southampton and propelled by a 33 h.p. PP Kelvin engine. About the same time she started ferrying on demand coach parties from Oban to Mull. The Catholic faith was for twenty-six years maintained on Mull thanks to Mrs Spencer conveying priests without fail every Sunday.

Henrietta's apprenticeship in boats commenced long before the last war when she was helping her father on his fishing boats operating from Croggan pier in the mouth of Loch Spelve on Mull. With the outbreak of the war she was carrying materials for an RAF installation on Kerrera. She was also involved in piloting, often being called out to guide some of the largest ships into Oban harbour. In the summer of 1940 she did not suffer gladly her small ferry *The Jean* being commandeered for the Dunkirk rescue operation. The Admiralty won but proving that she and her family were a force to be reckoned with Mrs Spencer bought *The Anna* from old Hughie Carmichael

Henrietta Spencer

of Craignure, father of the late Hughie Carmichael we knew in the 1960s and '70s, on condition that the RAF screened her so that she could not be taken away. That 30-ft open boat had been built by MacQueens at Easdale.

Amongst the bigger boats Mrs Spencer or her family commanded on ferrying to Mull and sometimes to Lismore, Kerrera and other destinations, was *Island Lass* a 45-ft by 14-ft 6-in mahogany planked launch built by Crinan Boatyard and powered by a Kelvin R4 70 h.p. diesel engine, and *Berbena*, a 40-ft launch with a Kelvin Ricardo PP engine. That one was acquired from Duncan Newlands, the well-known coxwain of the Campbeltown lifeboat.

The *Island Lass* was washed off the slipway at Crinan Boatyard during the hurricane of 1968 while undergoing annual survey there. Mrs Spencer was not compensated because the insurers called the incident 'an act of God'. The damage would have been covered were it caused by negligence.

Amongst Henrietta's distinguished passengers on their way to Mull, who in time became her friends, were Lord and Lady Maclean of Duart. She also used to ferry the Rab Butlers and the Harold Macmillans and plied her boats for James Mason's film-making. Henrietta's weatherbeaten walnut-like face and the kind of blue eyes which scan distant horizons made her look

The *Island Lass*

every inch the gallant sailor she was, her gallantry having been displayed in a number of marine rescue operations. Her fearlessness was proverbial: a tale used to go round Oban harbour of two women whom she undertook to ferry across to Grass Point in pretty rough weather. Once at sea the two passengers in fear and overcome by tears pleaded with Henrietta to turn back, but she was determined to fulfil the contract and delivered her charges safely to Mull. Grannie Spencer, as she came to be affectionately known in her native Oban, retired in 1985 at the age of eighty-seven after fifty years of stalwart ferrying service and received the Good Citizen of the Year award.

Although I had the privilege of knowing Henrietta Spencer professionally over many years I owe much of the information about her to her shipmates, her daughter Bella and her son-in-law Donald.

Ulva

The earliest mention of Ulva ferry in Provisions of the Commissioners of Supply for Argyll is dated 1747, when the inhabitants of Ulva were required to work for three days on the road upon the Mull side of the Ulva ferry and leading to it, between Killiemor and Oskamul. In 1773 Johnson and Boswell visited Ulva, and Boswell recorded:

> a servant was sent forward to the ferry, to secure the boat for us: but the boat was gone to the Ulva side, and the wind was so high that the people could not hear him call; and the night so dark that they could not see a signal. We should

Henrietta Spencer

have been in a very bad situation, had there not fortunately been lying in the little Sound of Ulva an Irish vessel [which] ferried us over.

Ulva ferry is perhaps best known for its part in Thomas Campbell's poem 'Lord Ullin's Daughter':

A chieftain of the Highlands bound
Cried Boatman do not tarry
And I'll give thee a silver pound
To row us over the ferry!

The author Thomas Campbell tutored the children of a Maclean family on a farm between Dervaig and Calgary; he later became Rector of Glasgow University, Poet Laureate and was buried in Westminster Abbey in 1844.

In 1862 the Ulva ferryman appears to have been Joseph Macdonald, who was also holding an inn and a merchant's store at the Sound of Ulva. The

The Mull–Ulva ferry

landlord of the island, Francis William Clark of Ulva House, wrote in that year to Nisbet Esq., Solicitor of Tobermory, 'be pleased to serve a summons of removing against Joseph Macdonald Innkeeper Sound of Ulva at my instance as landlord, to flit and remove at the approaching term of Whitsunday from Inn and Merchant Store and Ferry at the Sound of Ulva with the land and islands thereto attached'.

In 1874 – twelve years later – Francis W. Clark of Ulva House had to repeat his instruction, this time to Sproat and Cameron, Solicitors in Tobermory, maintaining that the ferryman/innkeeper had no lease, having the subjects only from year to year 'on tacit relocation'. I wonder how many more summonses had Mr Clark to issue? He was himself a solicitor from Stirling who decided on a radical reduction in the number of tenants and conversion of part of their grazing to a sheep farm. On the north side of Ulva the roofless houses of 'Starvation Terrace' stand as a stark reminder of Clark's policies. When he cleared part of the island for a sheep farm some of the victims moved to this area; others departed.

From the 1909 Return by the Mull District Committee one gathers that in that year Francis William Clark was still the laird but the ferryman was Malcolm MacPhail. Ulva Ferry was described as connecting the main road from Salen to Torloisk with the public road passing through the island of Ulva to the island of Gometra. The distance between landing places was shown as 200 yards. There were three boats serving the ferry, of 18 ft, 13 ft and 12 ft in length, and the passenger fare was tuppence.

Today the 24-ft outboard propelled blunt bowed ferry boat to Ulva still leaves from a pier on the north side of the Sound of Ulva. The ferry house is on the island so the ferry has to be summoned by sliding a board to reveal a large, red panel, which can be seen from the other side.

Mull to Lismore

There must have been at least a Sunday ferry from Mull to Lismore while Lismore was the seat of the Diocese of Argyll between 1200 and 1507. The earliest recorded reference to a ferry between Mull and Lismore I found is dated 1752. In that year John Campbell of Fiart on Lismore petitioned the Commissioners of Supply for Argyll to establish a regular ferry (see Chapter 8). In the early nineteenth century list of nine small Mull ferries there is one plying between Ardchoirk in Loch Don near Duart on Mull to Fiart on Lismore.

15

PORT ASKAIG TO FEOLIN

Port Askaig stands on the east coast of Islay, looking across the narrows of the Sound of Islay to Feolin on Jura's west coast. Sheltered from the west by cliffs on the Islay side and from the east by Jura's hills, it is one of the very few harbours on the coast of Islay which are safe in most weathers. Only when a north-easterly funnels down the Sound do ships have to shift their anchorages across to Whitefarland Bay on Jura.

The tide runs fast in the narrows – it can race to 5 knots – and to an untutored eye, the course of the ferry boat can be baffling. Starting from Feolin, the boat charges about half a mile upstream from Port Askaig, only to be carried crab-wise by the current to its proper destination. The crossing calls for ferrymen of great skill. Such were the MacPhee brothers, Peter and Archie, who was commonly known as 'The Gordie': a pair of incomparable boatmen, and respectively the coxswain and the mechanic of the first Islay lifeboat. Between them, they worked the ferry from Port Askaig for nearly half a century.

On the ferry, Peter was in command, and Archie was the mate and chief engineer. Peter was a man of few words and stuck to his Gaelic. Passengers' enquiries, when granted Peter's nodding permission, had to be addressed to The Gordie, who could usually be coaxed to translate the question and answer. The questioner would then perhaps be initiated into one of the mysteries of the Sound.

The ferrymen's fare structure was as unique as their knowledge of the Sound: usually 2s 6d for a local, but a tweedy gentleman in a deerstalker would be assessed as an 'English tourist' and be charged £1. Should he be so misguided as to sport a kilt as well as a deerstalker, he would be classed as a 'toff' and perhaps billed 30s. The MacPhees were no respecters of persons of rank, not even those 'of the cloth'. It has been said that a 'wee free' minister, church-bound from Islay to Jura, had to spend the night on the wrong side of the Sound because he protested that his conscience did not allow him to handle money on the Sabbath.

Archie and Peter resided on the Port Askaig side of the narrows, Archie in the Rock House, literally tucked into the cliff protecting the harbour from

Postcard of Port Askaig in the 1960s

the west, and Peter in a small cottage in the next bay, known as 'Freeport', a few hundred yards to the north. Other than at scheduled times, the ferry had to be summoned by phoning Rock House, whose number was, conveniently, Port Askaig 200. Holidaymakers renting the ferry cottage at Feolin, which was some ten miles from the nearest telephone, had to adopt other means of communication. Alastair Borthwick, a Scottish journalist and broadcaster, told me that Feolin ferry cottage was his home for the first year of his married life. When a small expansion of his family became imminent, he arranged with Archie a signal flag system to be used in an emergency. The prospective father kept running out of cigarettes as tension mounted, and on two successive evenings he hailed the ferry to get him to the Port Askaig shop in a hurry. When the flag went up on the third day, the brothers took their time to respond, and the little newcomer had to be given a do-it-yourself reception on Jura instead of being delivered in the comfort of Islay Cottage Hospital.

The MacPhees operated two motorboats. The larger one much resembled a standard 24-ft ship's motor lifeboat and bore the name *Rothesay Castle*. (The fact that a Union Castle cargo ship of that name went aground in the Sound of Islay soon after the Second World War is, of course, a coincidence!) The *Rothesay Castle* replaced the *Tritonia*, herself salvaged from a wreck on the Atlantic coast of the island. The smaller ferry boat, the *Kilroy*, carried a mast and a lug sail, which The Gordie maintained was the most efficient form of lifesaving gear: 'She's bound to be blown to one shore or the other', he would say to me when I tackled him on lifesaving equipment.

There was something of a special relationship between The Gordie and the Board of Trade Marine Survey Service in the person of the author. The Gordie could never produce the distress rockets he should have carried on board, his standard excuse being that they were classed as explosives and as such could not be sent by post. In the end, I was shamed into buying a set myself, and presented it to Archie on stepping off the motorship *Lochiel* at Port Askaig pier one day. He was not unduly effusive in his thanks, but a note was slid under my cabin door on the *Lochiel* that night. It requested me to pick up a 'wee brown parcel' which would be left outside Rock House before the *Lochiel*'s departure at 9 a.m. next morning. I was not to bother 'himself' at that unearthly hour. The parcel turned out to be a huge jute sack, the shape of which suggested it contained a leg of venison, with which I had to trudge up the *Lochiel*'s gangway. In response to whispered enquiries, I whispered in confidence that I had friends on the island who kept deer in their back garden.

On another occasion, I tried to impress on Archie the importance of having firefighting gear in the ferry boats. Next morning, I was awoken at the Port Askaig Hotel by cries that MacBrayne's cargo vessel, the *Loch Dunvegan,* was on fire. She was belching out smoke as she was heading up Islay Sound towards Rubha a' Mhàil point. Somewhere up there, Captain Watson must have come to the conclusion that it might be prudent to jettison the deck consignment of petrol drums, and did so. He also decided to turn the ship round and seek help alongside Port Askaig pier. Just then, Donnie Carmichael's bus came round to take me to MacBrayne's morning sailing from Port Ellen to Gourock, and to my social engagement in Glasgow that night. That was not to be, because a wiry arm seized me as I was about to climb aboard: 'Yesterday you were preaching on firefighting, now you'd better show us how to put out a real ship's fire!' The Gordie said with glee.

There was nothing for it but to stay and to call for the big trailer fire pump from Islay's Machrie Airport. A while later, the small Loganair aircraft carrying MacBrayne's marine and engineer superintendants to the emergency had to circle overhead without a hope of being allowed to land, because the airport now had no fire pump.

The fire was well and truly out by the evening, when Archie and his wife, Christine, embarked in one of the ferry boats to head up the Sound towards Rubh a'Mhàil. 'Where are you bound for?' I shouted. 'Bound on a social occasion' came the MacPhees' retort. Rumour had it that The Gordie didn't buy a gallon of petrol for his car for many months after. The rumour was reinforced by Richard Blair, who was a boy at the time of his father's death at Barnhill on Jura in 1950 and moved to his uncle's farm at Craignish, where they had a small boat for moving sheep. He remembers that sometime in 1960, after the Loch Dunvegan fire, 'We rescued about 3 drums of petrol we found floating about – mostly around Corrievrachan and the Dorus Mhor. Although they had to be shared with co-conspirators I don't think we bought any petrol for a long time.'

Until quite late in the eighteenth century, haymaking was uncommon in the Western Isles, which made it necessary for a large proportion of livestock to be disposed of each autumn. In 1772, it was estimated that 1,700 cattle were ferried from Islay to Jura. Statistics for the years 1801–7 show that the average annual number rose to 2,600. The Port Askaig–Feolin crossing then became a crucial link in the drove route from Islay via Jura to the mainland. Feolin boasted one of the four changehouses of Jura, the others being at Lagg, Kinuachdrach and Corran. Feolin pier, a mighty granite creation of 1810, with ramps on either side and a cattle enclosure, still stands solid, bearing testimony to its importance in bygone days. It is ascribed to Thomas Telford, but it was probably built to the plans of one James Hollinsworth, a civil engineer at Crinan, who modified an earlier design by David Wilson, a road engineer in Lochgilphead.

In 1787, Islay drovers asked for a fank to enclose their beasts while waiting for the ferry at Port Askaig. In that year, one was established on 60–80 acres, which indicates the size of the droves. At the end of that century, the ferry tenant was ordered not only to keep the stone slipway in order, to prevent cattle tripping, but also to 'adjudicate in disputes between drovers as to priority in getting on the ferry'. In 1824, a traveller described the noisy scene at the Port Askaig ferry and concluded that whisky did not tend to diminish the hustle and vociferation among the drovers and the boatmen. This is worthy of note because, only six years earlier, the local stent (excise) committee did away with the unlimited issue of whisky to ferrymen on account of 'the surplus quantity being often injurious to the cattle and proprietors thereof'. The allowance was fixed at 1 mutchkin (an English pint) for every thirty cattle ferried.

At the end of the nineteenth century, there was still a rowing ferry running from the Feolin as well as from the Islay side, the last ferryman being one James Sutherland. He lived in the Feolin ferry house, which still stands and is shown in the recent sketch, and marked his initials 'J.S.' and the date '1886' on the northern ramp of the Feolin pier. I understand that he died in 1919.

It would be a pity to mention the name of James Sutherland without quoting the story of 'James of the Shilling' associated with him, which appeared in *The Long Road, a Guide to Jura*, edited by Peter Youngson.

> In the days when Sutherland rowed the Feolin Ferry, he shared the job with McPhee of Port Askaig. The fare at the time was one shilling to cross.

An eighteenth-century print of the Sound of Islay (loaned by Norman Tait)

Now there was a Jura man who seemed loth to pay the fare. He would be quickly out of the boat as it came to land – tossing a coin over his shoulder into the bottom of the boat, and when the ferryman picked up the coin it would always turn out to be a Sixpence, not a Shilling. From which they took to calling the man Sheumais an t'shilling – James of the Shilling.

The Jura ferryman was a mild mannered man, and did not relish trouble of any kind, and so made no comment on the behaviour of this passenger, but the Islay man was less tolerant. 'The next time he wants to cross, let me have the ferrying of him,' he said.

So it was that he took the oars when James next appeared. He rowed halfway across the Sound, then he shipped one of the oars, and, lifting the other oar high above his head with both hands, he shouted 'Paidh a nis – Pay Now!'

And on that crossing Sheumais an t'shilling paid the fare in full.

In the mid-1960s a 100-ft long steel landing-craft, the *Isle of Gigha,* managed by John Rose, a sailor/engineer/enterpreneur, started to trade around Islay as a freelance vehicle ferry. Archie didn't take kindly to this intrusion, and in order to stop John Rose using the Feolin slip, one weekend he cemented in solid iron spikes so that the landing-craft's ramp could not be lowered. Come Monday morning, when John Rose, with the *Isle of Gigha,* swept round the point and saw the situation, without hesitation he lowered the heavy ramp and sheared off the spikes.

In 1966, the *Isle of Gigha* capsized on a passage from Gigha to Islay with the loss of two lives and four lorries. The salvaged vessel was made less likely to turn turtle by the erection of buoyancy tanks on deck, port and starboard,

The remains of a skiff ferry at Freeport, Port Askaig

under the watchful eye of the Board of Trade. Renamed the *Sound of Gigha*, she returned to service under the flag of Western Ferries, a company newly formed by a few enthusiastic directors of Harrison's Clyde shipowners, who in turn engaged enthusiastic crews. The aim was to give the islanders their first vehicular ferry service and to lower fares by introducing competition. Caledonian MacBrayne was certainly shaken out of its monopoly-induced complacency.

Following the demise of Peter and the retirement of Archie in 1969, the *Sound of Gigha* – dressed in Western Ferries' red-and-white colours and irreverently christened by The Gordie *Sgadan Dearg* ('Red Herring') – took up the run between Islay and Jura, this time as a drive-on-drive-off ferry. She happily plied across those narrows with passengers and vehicles for more than twenty years. The service has grown vastly in importance since Caledonian MacBrayne discontinued their direct sailings to Jura, leaving the Port Askaig–Feolin ferry as the only means of transport to that island. So it is likely to remain, unless the periodically resuscitated idea of an 'overland' route to Islay via a short crossing between Keills on the mainland and Lagg on Jura ever comes to fruition.

At the time of writing the Port Askaig to Feolin Crossing is being run by Serco Denham of Glasgow with an Argyll and Bute District-owned purpose built ferry which can carry eight cars. It seems to be fairly busy commercially since new regulations require the effluent from the Jura distillery to be carried by tankers to Islay. Since her introduction the new ferry has had some technical difficulties and her sailings are restricted in strong north and south winds and extreme tidal conditions.

Long after his retirement, The Gordie could be seen in his 'Para Handy' cap on Port Askaig pier, chatting with one of his friends, be it one of the Astors of Jura, Fraser, Lord Margadale's keeper, or Willy 'Fish', the Islay lifeboat mechanic; or he could be overheard muttering under his breath to those on the bridge of a Caledonian MacBrayne or Western Ferries ship manoeuvring to make landfall at Port Askaig: 'Give me the telegraph here and I will bring her in.'

16
TIREE AND COLL

The rich grazings of the islands of Tiree and Coll have produced a
significant number of cattle for export since records began. The obvious
drove route to the mainland led via Mull, as this afforded the best chance of
grazing on the way and the shortest sea-passages. Estimates by Knox from
his *Tour Through the Highlands and Hebrides of 1786* put the number of cattle
sent annually from Coll at 400 and from Tiree at 500. According to the *New
Statistical Account* of that period, there were on Tiree some twenty open or
half-decked boats of 6–230 tons deadweight employed on carrying cattle
between Coll and Tiree, or between Coll or Tiree and Mull. The landing
place on Mull for the Coll or Tiree cattle is vaguely described as 'at the back
of Mull', but according to tradition, ferry landings took place in the tiny bay
of Kintra, at the north-western corner of the Ross of Mull.

In the 1805 *Report of the Commissioners for Highland Roads,* there is a
proposal to extend the Mull road to Kintra, where cattle from Iona and Tiree
were often landed. The drove route from it already led along the shores of
Loch Scridain, through Glen More to the Grass Point–Kerrera crossing (see
Chapter Eight) and the mainland sales. Cattle from Coll were also ferried
to Croig on the north shore of Mull, between Calgary and Dervaig, and
those from Tiree to Ulva Ferry (Lagganulva). Both these points were more
convenient for Salen Fair than Kintra Bay.

In 1801, five partners took equal shares in a ferry boat intended for the
Tiree-Mull service: the Duke of Argyll; his chamberlain on Tiree, Malcolm
MacLaurin; the innkeeper at Scarinish; John Sinclair, a merchant of
Tobermory; and the ferryman. The purchase was probably in response to
MacLean of Coll having just acquired a packet-boat to act as a ferry from Coll
to Mull. The ensuing correspondence between Malcolm MacLaurin and the
duke throws light on ferrying of the time between the islands of Coll, Tiree
and Mull.

In 1802, MacLaurin told the duke that MacLean of Coll 'gives very
favourable encouragement to his packet boat and his fare is very low', and
that the ferryman of the packet-boat received as remuneration 'the grazing
of 4 cows and followers and a large croft free of rent'. He tried to induce the

duke to grant a croft on easy terms to the ferryman at Scarinish, otherwise 'the people of Tiree will be induced to go to Croig in Mull via Coll'.

In November 1804, the chamberlain wrote to the duke regarding the ferries between Tiree and Coll:

> The factor has frequently had occasions to observe the bad effects of the small boats kept for the purpose of the ferry between Tyree and Coll, in which neither cows or horses can be ferried without throwing them down and tying them on their passage, a practice that often produces serious effects and at times the deaths of these animals. The ferryman on the Coll side will not alter the custom that was there when he got the tack, as it would subject him to the expense of keeping a proper large boat, but on the Tyree side there is no such restriction and relief would certainly be desired from this evil, which the factor begs to represent to your Grace.

The duke was not easily persuaded, as may be gathered from his reply of October 1805 (from the disparity of dates, it would appear that postal communication between Tiree and Inveraray was not of the speediest in the early 1800s):

> Instructions for the Chamberlain of Tiree 31st October 1805: It does not appear that there can be sufficient intercourse in transporting cattle from Tiree to Coll to defray the expense of providing and keeping a large boat. I cannot therefore at present interfere in the manner that is pointed at by the Chamberlain, but if he will give further information on the subject it shall be considered.

The duke might not have thought much of the demand for cattle transport between the two islands, but the ferry from Caoles at the west end of Coll to Caoles at the east end of Tiree did not just carry people but also male calves – a byproduct of the dairy industry on Coll – and cheese, its primary product.

Cattle were carried to and from Tiree in modified 'Fifies', up to 30 ft long, broad-beamed, broad-shouldered and ballasted with stones. Boats of this type were developed on Tiree and were still used there as recently as the 1960s. Prof. Donald Meek tells of his grandfather's boat, the *Peace and Plenty*, a half-decked 'Fifie' smack which, in the early part of this century, was sometimes used to take Tiree potatoes to the mainland and would come back carrying coal. In these boats of 28–30 ft length, at least half-a-dozen fully-grown cattle could be carried, and they would be driven aboard from a pier or *lamhraig*, a convenient 'ferry rock'. To reduce damage to the boat's timbers, the ballast stones were covered with bracken to provide a *farradh*, which not only protected the timbers, but also provided a foothold for the cattle. The usual *farradh* material such as birch twigs, osier (willow shoots) or heather, were not easily found on Tiree. Floor covering of this kind also served to absorb the cow dung.

While most of the Tiree boats used for ferrying cattle were of the single-sail, dipping-lug rig, before the First World War there were a few bigger Tiree-based craft, luggers, perhaps 50 ft long, and carrying about 50 tons. These were fitted with a bowsprit, had a foresail and maybe also a mizzen sail. The *Princess Louise,* a converted iron steam drifter, was reputed to have carried 104 bullocks from Tiree in the 1930s.

The boatmen of Tiree, particularly those from east-end harbours, became very skilled at ferrying cattle. They pursued their skill throughout the Western Isles. Hugh MacLean tells of John MacDonald, a well-known Tiree ferry skipper in the 1930s, whose fame owed as much to his seamanship as to his dog, who could reputedly buy newspapers and read them. Once a week, the labrador, Carlow, used to walk 1½ miles to Scarinish pier to buy and fetch John's *Oban Times.* Came the 1936 coronation, and Carlow did not turn up with the paper after the 4 p.m. steamer's arrival. As it was getting dark, John went along the road in search of his friend. After a time, he heard whimpering at the roadside. Carlow was in the dyke, so the story goes, complaining that he could not finish reading the coronation story because of the failing light.

The well-built Tiree smacks and skiffs were of larch on oak, fastened with rooved iron nails. Boatbuilding was well developed. In the early part of this century, boats were still being built by Neil MacIntyre at Scarinish (the yard was behind the present butcher's shop), by the MacDonalds of Milton, by the MacLarens of Cornaigmore and by the MacKinnons of Vaul, all of whose boats were highly regarded.

While the 30-ft Tiree smack is virtually extinct – the upturned hull of what was perhaps the last one can still be seen forming the roof of a shed at Mannal – her smaller sister, the 18/20-ft dipping-lug and double-ended shiff or *sgoth,* has survived to this day. The yet smaller open boats were called *geola mhór* or *geola bheag* (a dinghy), according to size.

The Tiree skiffs, with their very distinctive hull forms, were the maids of all work of the seafaring community of the east end of the island, where there are reasonable anchorages. Most families found use for one, not only for communication across the Sound of Gunna and for ferrying calves and cheese from Coll, but also for fishing and as general-purpose craft. Their usual dimensions were 18 ft length, 4 ft depth, 8 ft beam and 2 ft draft, with at least a 6 in keel. Among the surviving skiffs is the 120-year-old *Heatherbell,* a working boat of about 8 ft beam, built by the MacKinnons of Vaul. Another, the *Mayflower,* built some 100 years ago by Captain Donald MacDonald at Milton, is finer at the stern, has only a 7-ft beam, and is more a racing than a working boat. Then there is the *Jessie* and one or two newer ones. The photograph overleaf shows either the *Mayflower* or the *Jessie* being raced by a crew of three.

Mary or *Effie* discharging cargo at Caolas, Tiree, c. 1920 (loaned by D.E. Meek)

Tiree, being largely an island of rich machair (sandy pasture) grazing, has always been short of fuel. The small quantities of peat that could be found on the island were mostly of inferior quality. The most inferior was, according to Hugh MacLean, known as puisd. A slightly superior type was known as sgron. These peats could hardly qualify as fuel, and were instead used to thatch the poorest houses. The real peat, or moine had to be ferried over from Coll, or to a greater extent, from the Ross of Mull, a patch of which, west of Bunessan, traditionally 'belonged' to Tiree.

John and Calum MacLean, talking to Eric Cregeen in 1968, told of Tiree people having had peat concessions on the Ross of Mull, along the side of Loch Scridain. In the summer, they used to sail over in their open skiffs. Some got the use of a Mull pony, and some even brought their own pony in the skiff to take the peats down to the shore in panniers. Whole families used to go over to Mull, in spite of the dangerous stretch of open sea. John and Calum could think of only one tragedy, when boats from Balephuil capsized near the Mull shore in a freak storm. A Balephuil bard, Alasdair Mór, wrote a song about it.

Donald Sinclair of Tiree, when in his eighties, told Eric Cregeen of peat ferrying from Mull within his own memory. A 'sizeable' boat would go over from West Hynish pier to the Ross of Mull for moine with three families from Balephuil. When the peat was all stacked, the men would go home to carry on fishing, leaving the women behind to get the peat dry. He told of some of the boats capsizing and being lost due to overloading. Donald described the boats as being 18–20 ft long, with a main and a mizzen lug

The hull of a newer Tiree sailing skiff (loaned by Dr Arthur Kitchin)

sail, and West Hynish as a good pier, which could take horses and carts for unloading peat. Donald referred to the Tiree patch of the Ross of Mull as 'Blar mór nan Tirisdeach' ('the big peat bog belonging to Tiree'), and located it at Kintra – 'Ceann Traghaid' ('the head of the beach'). According to him, Tiree men did not have to pay for the peat they ferried; apparently, the duke used to settle the account with the Mull tenants.

Hugh MacLean of Barrapol, also in his eighties, talking to me in 1989, threw some doubt on the story of peat being ferried from Mull in Donald's lifetime. He said that his uncle, who emigrated to Canada in 1877, was ferrying coal to Tiree from the mainland before he left. In Hugh's youth, before the Second World War, a little peat, mainly local and from Coll, was burnt, but imported coal was the fuel in common usage.

In the early part of this century, coal was brought to Tiree and Coll mainly in Clyde puffers, but Tiree had also its own coal ferry, the *Mary Stewart*, a double-topsail schooner which belonged to Donald MacLean of Scarinish. When he could no longer sail the ship – her last crossing was in 1938 – Donald decided to let *Mary Stewart* die her natural death in preference to selling her. Her wood skeleton is a permanent feature of Scarinish Harbour today. From measurements of the wreck taken at low water, it would appear that she was about 72 ft long, had an 18-ft beam and that she probably carried about 90 tons of coal.

A Tiree skiff racing (loaned by Duncan Cameron)

The importance of the Tiree skiff probably began to decline when steamers started to call at Tiree and Coll, providing a regular communication between the two islands. However, the pier at Arinagour on Coll was not much favoured by steamers because lack of water caused blocked injections and allowed sand into the condensers. Hence, passengers, livestock and goods had to be transferred by a ship-to-shore ferry.

The Coll ship-to-shore ferrymen left behind them memories going back to the 1880s, when Charles MacFadyen, known as 'Tearlach Mór' ('Big Charles') had the job. He was not really a big man, but broad-chested, long in the back, short in the legs and very strong and hardy, just what was needed to row heavy, cumbersome boats in strong winds and rough seas. His skill in boat-handling, his special sense of finding the required landfall accurately, as well as his prowess, were highly regarded by the captains of the mail steamers calling at Arinagour ('Airidh-nan-Gobhar', the 'Shieling of the goats'). The reproduction of one of the contemporary postcards shows one of Charles's ferry boats, known as the 'black boat', carrying twenty passengers, several sheep, three head of cattle and a horse. She is rowed by two men with long oars. One of them would be Tearlach, the paid ferryman. The other could have been one of his sons, the postman or a local man who had come to meet his mainland friends or relatives arriving off the steamer. Tearlach Mór

Tearlach Mór's 'black boat' (loaned by Captain and Mrs Robertson)

carried on ferrying until shortly before his death at the age of seventy-six in 1919.

Tearlach Mór was succeeded by John MacDonald, known as 'Ian Dhomhuill Thearlaich'. In stature and strength, he was not unlike his predecessor. He was the first ferryman to take charge of a motor ferry, one that was sold to MacBrayne's by Commander MacEwan of the Isle of Muck in 1935. The motorboat was similar in design to a 45-ft naval pinnace. The engine was enclosed in a cabin of sufficient headroom to allow ferrymen to attend to it in an unrestricted posture. The after-end of the cabin was sheltered from heavy weather coming from astern by a half-bulkhead, so that the mechanic could operate the throttle and gear lever while sitting on the bulkhead and being in communication with the ferrymaster at the tiller. A short foredeck protected the forward well, which could carry horses, cattle or sheep.

The rowing ferries were not dispensed with for some years. They were used to expedite the discharge of cargo while the motor ferry pressed on with landing passengers and mail before returning to the ferry to assist the rowing boats to the shore. Tearlach Mór's rowing 'black boat', which originally belonged to MacCallum Orme, came to grief in 1956, when, having loaded copper pipes for a new housing scheme on the island, she split in two and sank, thankfully without loss of life. The cargo of pipes became a hazard to steamers in Loch Eatharna, as they frequently moved with storm surge, fouling ships' anchors. It took good seamanship to stop a vessel from drifting onto a lee shore, while her anchor was being cleared.

John MacDonald was a unique individual. A first-class boatman by nature

John MacDonald and the Coll View girls, 1920s

and upbringing, he also had a working knowledge of the stock exchange and
an interest in it. He could not have been without social graces, because he was
known to attract female attention. He died a bachelor, although a number
of island and mainland ladies would not have turned down his proposal.
During the years he was in charge of MacBrayne's ferries, including the big
red rowing ferry, a group of young schoolteachers from the mainland used
to come to Arinagour in the summer. Throughout their holiday, they were
John's constant companions, rowing the ferry boat and generally making
themselves useful to him. He loved their company without surrendering his
freedom.

John MacDonald's pony was almost as much of a character as the
ferrymaster himself. It and Dr Paterson's pony used to stand for hours, head
to head, whispering into each other's ears. They were objects of much interest
to visitors to Coll in the 1930s. John MacDonald's pony possessed more than
usual intelligence. It could undo the latch of any gate and gain access to
something more dainty than ordinary pasture.

John MacKinnon – 'Ian Dhonnchaidh' – took over from John MacDonald
as ferrymaster. He had served in the Dover Patrol in the First World War, and
he was on HMS *Vindictive* while she took part in the Zeebrugge operations.
The raid was unsuccessful, and eventually the order was given to scuttle the
ship at Zeebrugge so as to block the submarines and fast torpedo boats
within their base. The crew were instructed to remain on board their sinking
vessel until picked up by motor launches. While waiting on the deck of the

Vindictive under shellfire, Ian Dhonnchaidh spotted a nice sheave block (pulley) in the rigging and thought it would be a waste for it to go down with the ship while it could perform useful work on a skiff in Coll. He climbed the rigging, cut off the block and took it home to Coll on his next leave.

After John MacKinnon, the ferry passed to Hugh MacKinnon – 'Eoghainn Sheumais Alasdair' – whose brother, 'Lachuinn Ruadh' or Lachy, worked for a time on the Bonawe ferry plying across Loch Etive (see Chapter Eleven). Hugh left the ferry partly because of the management's reluctance to replace the ageing engine of the 'grey boat'. Eventually the 'grey boat' broke up when she drifted ashore near Caolas an Eilein due to engine failure. Ironically, she had her replacement engine on board.

The replacement for the 'grey boat' was a red motorboat built to the order of MacBrayne's, an improved 'grey boat' design. She was named Coll, and remained on station until the new pier was commissioned in 1960.

Prior to the introduction of the vehicle ferries in the 1970s, the MacBrayne motorship *Claymore* used to run on a two-day turn-around schedule from Oban to Coll and Tiree, on to Castlebay, Barra and Lochboisdale, South Uist, and calling again at Tiree and Con on the return journey. For many years, the master of the *Claymore* was Captain Donald Gunn, and his mate was John Lamont, a 'landowner' of Tiree. I happened to be on the ship's bridge one day, and just as we were going through the Sound of Gunna, between Tiree and Coll, I noticed John Lamont peering through the binoculars. 'Are you finding your way through the rocks of the Sound?' I asked the mate. 'Not at all,' interjected the captain, 'he is counting the cows on his farm!'

At the time of writing, Caledonian MacBrayne's latest passenger and vehicle motor ferry, the *Lord of the Isles,* calls at Scarinish and Arinagour terminals four days a week, with Arinagour having two calls each day. Vehicles are rolled on and rolled off with the help of the linkspan which was constructed at Arinagour in 1991. Most supplies are ferried in and cattle ferried out by road transport. Both Coll and Tiree people can be ferried to the other island on the four days of call each week.

17

WEST LOCH TARBERT

Before rough tracks grew into roads and cars became an everyday means of transport, West Loch Tarbert, which now forms a barrier between Knapdale and Kintyre, was a channel of communication between them. This is well illustrated by the linked parishes of Kilberry and Kilcalmonnell, which straddle the loch, and which were linked from before the Reformation until 1965. One priest and one minister served congregations on both sides of the loch. The Kilberry people – who were without a church building until 1821, when the present Kilberry parish church was built at Largnahension at the head of Loch Stornoway – were ferried across the loch to Kilcalmonnell church in Clachan at communion times. Already by 1560 Kilberry had been linked to Kilcalmonell across West Loch Tarbert, and services took place when weather permitted the crossing.

The two ferries spanning the loch's shores were part of a long-established route from the north to Campbeltown and Islay. At Ormsary, the route offered a choice. One route led by the coast road over Kilberry Head to the one mile ferry crossing from Ardpatrick to Portachoillan (Clachan). Until the last quarter of the eighteenth century, that coast road was the only land linked between the Kintyre peninsula and the rest of Argyll. A map of 1776 marks 'a new road now making' – the difficult *'Sliabh Gaoil'* route along Loch Fyne's shore, which was prompted by Campbell of Stonefield, and which is now followed by the A83. The other route led over the high ground to Avinagillan – that track is now no longer continuous – for the Dunmore–Kilchamaig (Whitehouse) ferry, a crossing of just over half a mile. The 1775 official record designates the Dunmore ferry as 'Kintyre Ferry Number 1' and the Ardpatrick ferry as 'Kintyre Ferry Number 2'.

The two ferries were in existence a long time before the official ferry records began on the order of the Argyll Commissioners in 1775. The first mention of the Dunmore ferry I have found goes back to 1689, when Jacobite supporters of Macneill of Gallachoilly, Macdonald of Largie and MacAllister of Loup crossed by Dunmore ferry to face William of Orange's troops from Ayr, who landed at Tarbert, Loch Fyne. After the Battle of Loup, the Jacobites scattered. Some took themselves to Gigha, and some were rescued by boats from Mull.

The death of the last of the Macmillans of Dunmore in a drowning accident in 1720 might suggest that the small Dunmore ferry was operated by that family up to that date. The drowning appears to have been caused by a dog starting a fight on a ferry boat loaded with wedding guests.

I came across a relic concerning the Ardpatrick ferry, which dates to the early part of the seventeenth century, when the MacAllisters of Loup ran it from both sides. The coats of arms of the MacAllister of Loup (a salmon) and of the Campbell of Kilberry (the *Galley of Lorn*), dated 1620, are carved on a stone forming the door lintel of the shed at Portachoillan, which might have been the old ferry house or ferry 'waiting room'. The stone could have been carved to celebrate a MacAllister–Campbell wedding which possibly gave control of the ferry. Was this the ferry house which, towards the end of the eighteenth century, was reputed to have been an illicit pub for the benefit of the ferry travellers, with one Charles Stuart as an innkeeper? Alternatively, is that inn represented by the ruins in the garden of the present ferry house?

In 1747, James MacAllister, the Factor of Loup, was requested by the Commissioners of Supply to employ as many of the tenants of the Loup Estate 'as he shall judge reasonable to work at repairing the keys' on both sides of the Ardpatrick ferry. The ferry was shown as a working one on General Roy's map of about 1750.

One Sunday in 1788, the Kilberry people were to travel to Kilcalmonnell church for communion. An unholy row blew up when they sailed in their own boats round Ardpatrick Point and landed in Dunskeig Bay, thus saving the fare on the Loup ferry between Ardpatrick and Portachoillan and having a shorter distance to walk to communion at the church in Clachan.

The ferry owner, MacAllister of Loup, who was an elder of Kilcalmonnell church, left his post at the church door to go down to move their boats across the loch, and then lay in wait for the Kilberry families trudging to his ferry on their way home, with a stout stick in his hand. He later tried to sue some of the Kilberry people for stealing timber from Ardpatrick, where he managed plantations belonging to the Duke of Argyll, but the case was dropped when it became clear that every witness intended to speak out about the ambush after communion in order to prove malice.

From about 1800, the ferry based on the Portachoillan side was run by three generations of MacPhails. Malcolm and his son, John, ferried until about 1860, and Malcolm's grandsons, Neil and John, worked the ferry for fifty-five years until 1915. Their brother-in-law, Duncan MacDougal, carried on until 1922, with the professional assistance of Mrs Grace MacDougall, née MacPhail. Their nephew, Ian MacPhail, lived at Clachan and Duncan MacDougall still lived in Tarbert at the time of writing.

On the Ardpatrick side John Leitch was the ferryman from 1823 till 1850. He must have been a 'man o'pairts', a person of some standing in the neighbourhood. In addition to being recorded as ferryman he was noted as local schoolmaster around 1840. In some documents he is referred to as innkeeper and also as farmer. It is understood that there was 6 acres of land that 'went' with the ferry house. Presumably all these additional duties would have helped feed his family of eight children during the 1840s, a period of very poor harvests in that part of Scotland. As ferryman he would be an agent of the heritor, probably of Campbell of Kilberry, and would employ or contract oarsmen. John's sudden death in 1850, when his eldest sons were still in their teens, led to his widow and family leaving Ardpatrick.

From the manuscripts found in Kilberry (Leargnahension) church one can gather grains of information on the ferry traffic. In August 1823 a sum of 10d was paid to John Leitch, presumably by the session clerk: 'To 2 gills liquor in time of ferrying the tent by Don McPhail, John McKillop etc.' And in June 1825, 'To ferrying the tent 1s and 10d to 2 gills liquor by A Galbreath, Don McPhail etc.' McPhail, McKillop and Galbreath were probably John Leitch's oarsmen. It would appear that whisky might have been part of the bargain for rowing the tent across or perhaps a reward for porterage of the tent on either side.

The 'tent' was, it seems, an important piece of equipment, conveyed by ferry back and forth between Kilcalmonnel and Kilberry as it was needed, according to the notes exhibited in Kilberry church by the late Miss Marion Campbell.

It was not a marque to accommodate a congregation but a portable pulpit to shelter the preacher and his books. It was used for Communion when a very large congregation assembled and before the church was built at regular services. According to Alaistair Phillips in his book *My Uncle George* the tent was a wooden, sacking-covered (probably sailcloth in this case) frame the shape and size of a Punch & Judy box, with a brass hook for the preacher to hang his watch on. The worshipers were unlikely to have seen Punch & Judy shows or they might have noticed the resemblance. A tent was made for the church in 1827 by Archibald Leitch, for which the session clerk paid him £5. Archibald was perhaps a kinsman of the ferryman.

It is understood that prior to the parish changes in the twentieth century the three o'clock services at Kilberry were to suit the ferry crossings, after the minister had conducted his service south of the Loch.

Still on the Ardpatrick side, the bachelor MacAllister brothers were ferrying from the middle of the nineteenth century until 1920, supplementing that income with lobster fishing. They were renowned for the brass bugle with which one of them would call the other when he happened to be on the Portachoillan side with the boat.

The 1891 *Schedule of Ferries* describes the Ardpatrick–Portachoillan ferry fleet as consisting of clinker-built rowing and sailing boats of 15–18 ft keel,

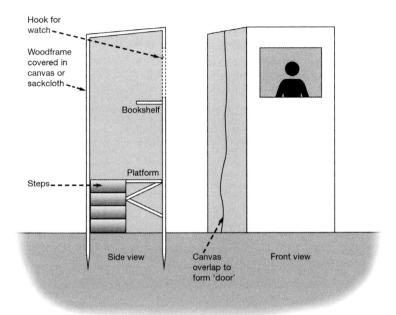

Hook for
watch

Woodframe
covered in
canvas or
sackcloth

Bookshelf

Platform

Steps

Side view

Canvas
overlap to
form 'door'

Front view

The tent, based on a sketch in *My Uncle George* by Alastair Philips (Pan Books, 1984)

which could take up to 1 ton of weight, and 14-ft rowing boats. The list of charges gives one an idea of what was carried: 'a very small pony' appears to have been the only regular horse-traveller – it might have been the minister's steed. Cows and bulls were carried for 1 to 2s each, and calves and pigs for 3 to 6d. Unaccompanied bags and parcels were also charged at 3–6d, unless they weighed over 1 cwt, when they cost 1s each, as did barrels. Furniture removal was subject to a private arrangement with the ferryman. The passenger fare was 1s, but if there were more than one in a party, they paid 6d each. On the smaller Dunmore ferry, 6d was the standard passenger fare.

The ferrymen on both crossings were nearly always part-time. In 1877, the following advertisement appeared in the *Argyll Advertiser*: 'Wanted for Ardpatrick West Loch Tarbert a good shoemaker, who would also undertake the charge of a ferry.' In 1908, the ferryman, who was also the tenant of Portachoillan Farm, complained to his ferry owner: 'Time lost to farm work, especially in fine weather, was not adequately compensated for by ferry remuneration.' The ferry owner to whom the complaint was made was Duncan MacKinnon, the heir to Sir William MacKinnon, the laird of Balnakill and owner of the Portachoillan ferry for most of the second half

Portchoillan ferry house with Sir William's window (loaned by Dr Arthur Kitchen)

of the nineteenth century, who founded the British East Africa Company. However, he must have had some spare time to keep an eye on the activities of the Portachoillan ferry, because he had his own private window fitted in the ferry house for that purpose.

A complaint similar to that made in 1908 was made 104 years earlier, when the owner of the Ardpatrick Estate, a Campbell of Shawfield, petitioned the Road Trustees for an increase in the ferry dues at Ardpatrick, where the ferryman was entitled to only a small share of the dues paid. Campbell of Shawfield acquired the (forfeited) Ardpatrick Estate from Angus MacAllister of Loup's Trustees in 1796. His descendants, three admirals, were the successive owners of the estate and of the ferry (1850–1920).

At the turn of the century and between the wars, the Dunmore ferry was owned by the absentee Fraser-Campbells. Argyll County Council took some interest in it from the 1920s onward. They seem to have paid little attention to the pier, but built a ferryman's house, now called 'Tigh-na-Leven'.

Turning to more recent times, Morris MacMurchie, who took over the Portachoillan tenancy from Duncan MacDougall, carried on from 1922 until 1952 and was the last ferryman from that side of the loch, although such ferrying as he did was increasingly to the Islay steamer, rather than across to Ardpatrick. An 18-ft boat was needed because of the volume of cargo in the form of draff from the Islay distilleries. Ian Macdonald, who came to Portachoillan in 1952, and at the time of writing lives at Clachan, remembers that the only time he ferried a passenger over to Ardpatrick was in 1954, when he took pity on a cyclist from Campbeltown and crossed with him in his 12-ft lobster boat.

Mr Thomson, his son Duncan, and the rest of the Thomson family of nine, started running the Ardpatrick ferry in the 1930s. Duncan Thomson, who at the time of writing lives in retirement near Dunmore, tells of a 16-ft fishing boat having been used alternately for lobster fishing and ferrying. A 22-ft lugsail skiff occasionally came into use.

Duncan recalls the severe winter of 1947, when he had to ferry the mail for Kilberry, Ardpatrick and Clachan and transfer groceries from the Islay steamer in mid-loch. Every second Sunday, he used to carry across Mr MacNab, the minister of Kilcalmonnell and Kilberry, and a native of Skye. The minister was still being ferried in the later 1940s, until he was presented with a car by Sir Robert MacAlpine. From time to time, Duncan ferried the itinerant blacksmith, who would adopt Knapdale as his base for a few days and work from farm to farm. It was in Duncan's time that the passenger fare rose to 1s and a new signalling system of waving a white towel was adopted. This seems to have been a technological simplification of the earlier system, which involved flagpoles on either side of the loch and which, in the end, was used mainly for shore-to-ship signalling. A hunting horn was also used.

Duncan Thomson had some anxious moments. When a 40-gallon drum of paraffin was thought too heavy for the boat, it was dropped overboard to be towed astern. It took so long to reappear that Duncan thought he would have to pay for it. It surfaced eventually and was towed to Corran pier at Portachoillan, destined for Ronachan Farm. Duncan's worst journey was when he had to ferry home the big cow his father had bought for £24. Ballast had to be removed from the bilges of the ferry boat *Alison* and the deck strengthened. The cow was gently haltered and lashed in the boat, and a sharp knife was held ready to release her in case she proved difficult. The boat rolled lazily without the ballast, and the cow rolled even more. Mrs Thomson was too anxious to watch the precarious proceedings, but in the end the cow was landed safely, and a calf was born next morning!

Duncan MacDougall could cast his mind back some seventy years to his father's days and to some of the tasks of the Portachoillan ferryman of that era. Old Dr Thomson, based on Clachan, had to be taken across to see Admiral Campbell and other patients in Knapdale. Until the Kilberry telegraph office was opened, telegrams had to be taken from the Clachan post office to the ferry by the postman on his bicycle, and the ferryman would deliver them to the Kilberry postman, who would set off on his bike. On one historic occasion, the coachman at Kilberry set off galloping towards the Ardpatrick ferry to send a telegram from Clachan to summon the Tarbert policeman to a fight between builders' men at Kilberry Castle. John Campbell of Kilberry stopped him at the church, rode back and settled the matter.

Ferry for the Islay steamer near Clachan in 1899 (loaned by the Scottish Ethnological Archive)

The Irish labourers working on drainage schemes in Kintyre were not averse to the hostelry at Largnahension at the head of Loch Stornoway, Clachan presumably being 'dry'. Such passengers could represent an awkward cargo when on bicycles: a 16-ft sailing boat stacked with bicycles needed all the ferryman's skill when a stiff south-westerly was blowing up the loch. One of the more regular customers of the Portachoillan and Dunmore ferries was the gauger (exciseman), heading from Kintyre towards a thatched cottage at Torinturk on the Knapdale side, in which an old man ran a small still. The tell-tale signal for passers-by was the ladder to the thatched roof – when this was in position, it meant that a dram was available.

The arrival of the Islay steamer in 1830 endowed the West Loch Tarbert ferries with a secondary function, which in time gave them 'bread-and-butter' employment increasingly more regular than that provided by the traffic across the loch. Since the road between Clachan and Tarbert – the present A83 – was in such poor condition that, at times, it was virtually non-existent until well into this century, and the Kilberry to Tarbert road was in a similar state, the steamer presented a speedy and well-appointed means of transport between Tarbert and townships on both sides of the loch. The Kilberry and Clachan people found it easier to take a ferry to the Islay steamer and thence travel to Tarbert in comfort than to struggle by coach. The ferries served as tenders, first to the *Glencoe,* then to the paddlesteamer *Pioneer,* and from the late 1930s on, to the motorship *Lochiel.*

There was a well-established system for directing the ferries. When a steamer needed a ferry on the Clachan side, a pennant was hoisted on that side of her mast, and when the Ardpatrick ferry was needed, the pennant went up on the other side; when both ferries were required, pennants went up on both port and starboard. Both the *Pioneer* and the *Lochiel* had a small crojack-yard on the foremast, on which the pennants were hoisted. Flagstaff Hill above Ardpatrick House served as a signal-point on the northern side, and presumably there was a similar facility on the other side.

In Ian Macdonald's times, in the early 1950s, the ferry house at Portachoillan was used as an unofficial lighthouse for the Islay steamer before a light was established at Corran Point later in the 1950s, following the *Lochiel's* grounding. A light in the porch allowed the *Lochiel* to check whether she was drifting when anchored, waiting for the ferry. There were times when the *Lochiel* found it safer to anchor off Ardpatrick.

Ian recollects his parents telling of an occasion during the First World War when they could not get seats on the Tarbert–Campbeltown coach. They sent a telegram to an uncle at Tayinloan asking him to meet them at Clachan. They then walked from East Loch Tarbert to West Loch Tarbert, embarked on the *Pioneer* and disembarked at Portachoillan, whence their uncle conveyed them in his sporty spring cart to Tayinloan.

Duncan Thomson also told of the trials and tribulations of transferring passengers, their luggage and bicycles between the shore and the Islay steamer. No line could be made fast aboard the *Pioneer* while the paddles were turning because of the turbulence they caused, so the ferry would drift in mid-loch, with passengers ready to board, positioned according to the wind so that the steamer, which was also drifting, provided a lee. When the *Pioneer* signalled by raising a flag, the passengers would be helped aboard smartly before the paddles started to turn again. It was a two-man operation: one ferryman attended to the unfastened rope and fended off, while the other helped passengers to get on board.

The ferries were also useful in shipping cargo for the farms on the southern side of the loch: cattle food, fertilizer, empty rabbit hampers from the mainland, and draff from the Islay distilleries to serve as animal fodder. The cargo from the mainland was loaded on a Caledonian MacBrayne cargo ship in the Clyde, taken to Islay, transhipped at Port Ellen onto the Islay steamer, and then onto the West Loch Tarbert ferry for Portachoillan. The 16-ft ferry could carry 1 ton, and that was a handy load for two carts. The ferry boat was beached on the sand beside the jetty, where the two horsedrawn carts could be backed into the sea, one on either side of the boat, until the water was up to the horses' bellies. Unloading the cargo into the carts allowed the boat to float into shallower water, and the carts could follow. Sometimes, the horses got a bit restless, and the cartwheels would sink into the sand. The horses were then hard put to drag the ½ ton load up the brae, to the road.

The Dunmore ferry was the first to come to an end, owing to lack of demand, around 1926. A story about the last Dunmore ferryman, Neil Hamilton, tells how he got very worried one night when his light picked out two eyes following him in the water. It took some time before he persuaded himself that it was a fox swimming the loch. The Portachoillan ferry gradually ceased as successive tenants became more farmers than boatmen. The pier at Portachoillan has not undergone major repairs since Sir William MacKinnon's days. The Ardpatrick ferry continued longest, into the 1950s, with Duncan Thomson in charge.

GLOSSARY

Ascog, Askaig	corruptions of Gaelic *aiseag* ('ferry'), commonly found as Scottish place-names (Norse settlers having hardened the former 'sh' sound to 'sk'). An alternative from the Norse is Ask-vik, meaning Ash tree bay.
boll	a relatively inaccurate measure of volume, varying from 1½ bushels in 1200 to 4 or 6 bushels in 1618. It was standardised as a measure of weight (140 lb) in 1696, but various Scottish counties still adhered to different standards, the most widely adopted being 6 bushels.
changehouse	small inn or alehouse
cobble	small, flat-bottomed barge
draff	malt waste from brewing, often used as cattle fodder
fank	sheep or cattle fold
gabbart	a nineteenth-century, double-ended sloop-rigged sailing lighter of about 40 ft length, used on the west coast of Scotland.
Glasgow Fair	traditional annual public holiday during the last two weeks of July. Many Glasgow businesses closed during this period, and it was customary to travel down the Clyde.
heritor	parish landholder, liable to pay tax and contribute towards public works, either by payment or labour
merkland	Scots measure of a piece of land's worth or area. Rent was traditionally paid in kind rather than cash, and the merk was one of the units of value (although merks were later coined as currency). A merkland was a unit of a land's productivity rather than a fixed area, until it was standardised at about 43 acres after 1585.
pound Scots	the pound Scots and the pound sterling were equal in value until about 1360. Thereafter, the pound Scots devalued

against sterling, and from 1601 until the Treaty of Union in 1707, £1 Scots was equal to 1s 8d sterling (although inflation due to debasement of coinage meant that the purchasing power of the pound Scots was then only ⅟₃₆ of its 1360 value).

stirk	young (or yearling) cow or bull
stock	twelve sheaves of corn
sweep	long oar, used on rowing ferries
tack	lease or tenure. To set property in tack was to let it to a tacksman.
tacksman	leaseholder, who held the tack on property and could sublet to others
tigh	Gaelic 'house'; in a geographical context usually means an inn
vernal birks	boat's floor covering, or *farradh* of spring birch twigs

WRITTEN SOURCES

Chapter One

Archives of the Heritage Museum at Brodick
Notes of Mr Robert Logan of Corrie
Notes by Capt. Edward Rawlence
Notes by Capt. Alaistair Sillan

Chapter Two

History of the County of Bute, J. E. Reid (Thos Murray Glazier, 1964)
'Bute Sketches', Jas. Duncan (The Buteman)
Scottish Field, December 1965
History of Our District, Kilchattan Bay S.W.R.I.
The Buteman, 25 May, 1 & 8 June, 5 October and 16 November 1956

Chapter Three

Colonsay and Oronsay, John de Vere Loder
Summer in the Hebrides, F. Murray
Hebridean Islands, Colonsay, Gigha, Jura, John Mercer (Blackie, Glasgow)

Chapter Four

'Memories of Luing over half a Century', Arthur Galbraith, *Luing Newsletter*,
    1980
Oban Times, 12.11.49, 18.3.61, 2, 5, 11 & 17.9.61, 24.8.89, 9.1.92
Scottish Daily Express, 16.3.61
Coastguard, January 1978
Notes by Mrs jean Baker

Chapter Five

The Story of Gigha: the Flourishing Island, Kathleen Philip
Gigha Sessions Book
Gigha Register of Births, Marriages and Deaths
Account of the State of Gigha Parish, Revd James Curdie
1792 and 1891 *Statistical Accounts*
Provisions of the Commissioners of Supply for Argyll

Chapter Six

Iona, The Living Memory of a Crofting Community 1750–1914, E. Mairi
    MacArthur (new pbk edition, Polygon at Edinburgh, 2000)
Columba's Island. Iona from Past to Present, E. Mairi MacArthur (Edinburgh
    University Press, 1995)
Tour of the Highlands and Western Islands, John Leyden (William Blackwood,
    Edinburgh, 1903)
'Diary of Charles Shaw-Lefevre', *Hampshire Chronicle,* 17.5.1991
Circuit Journeys, Henry Cockburn (Edinburgh, 1888)
*Remarks on Local Scenery and Manners in Scotland during the years 1799 and
    1800,* John Stoddart (London, 1801)
'The Highland Note Book', Robert Carruthers *(Inverness Courier,* July 1835)

Chapter Seven

Jura, an Island of Argyll, D. Budge (John Smith & Sons, Glasgow, 1960)
The Drove Roads of Scotland, A.R.B. Haldane (Nelson, 1952)
Highland Tours, J. Hogg (Byway Books, Hawick)
Hebridean Islands, J. Mercer (Blackie, 1974)
Reminiscences of my life in the Highlands, J. Mitchell (privately published,
    1883)
A Tour in Scotland, T. Pennant (White, 1776)
Register of Provisions of the Commissioners of Supply for Argyll
The Long Road: A Guide to Jura, Revd Peter Youngson (ed.)
Scotch and Water, Neil Wilson

Chapter Eight

Island of Kerrera, Miss H. MacDougall of MacDougall

Companion and Useful Guide to the Beauties of Scotland, Sarah Murray
   (Byway Books, Hawick, 1982)
Journal of a Tour to the Hebrides, James Boswell
Provisions of the Commissioners of Supply for Argyll

Chapter Nine

Provisions of the Commissioners of Supply for Argyll
Minutes of the Synod of Argyll

Chapter Ten

Notes of the research carried out by Mrs I. Crawford of Loch Awe, Lady M.
   McGrigor, FSA Scot. of Dalmally, and Mrs A. Rose of Kilchrenan, Argyll
   Archives
'Portsonachan Ferry', Lady M. McGrigor, FSA Scot., *The Kist** No. 43
'Portinnisherrich, Loch Awe', Lady McGrigor, FSA Scot., *The Kist** No. 45
Inveraray Castle Archives (with the help of Alastair Campbell of Airds and
   Mrs Rae MacGregor)
Schedule of Particulars as to Ferries, 1891
Argyll County Council's Report on Ferries, 1909
   History of Kilchrenan and Dalarich, Morag S. MacKay
   History of South Lochaweside
   History of South-East Lochaweside, Lady M. MacGrigor, FSA Scot.

Chapter Eleven

A Companion and Useful Guide to the Beauties of Scotland, Sarah Murray
   (Byway Books, Hawick, 1982)
Remarks on Local History and Manners in Scotland, John Stoddart (London,
   1801)
A Tour in Scotland 1803, Dorothy Wordsworth, J.C. Shairp (ed.) (James
   Thin, Edinburgh, 1974)
Schedule of Particulars as to Ferries, 1891
Argyll County Council's Report on Ferries, 1909
Review of Ferries, 1948

Chapter Twelve

A Tour in Scotland 1803, Dorothy Wordsworth, J.C. Shairp (ed.) (James
   Thin, Edinburgh 1974)

Notes of the research by Mrs Sheila MacIntyre of Creggans House and of the Inveraray Local History Workshop

Highland Tours in 1802 to 1804, James Hogg, with an introduction by Sir Walter Scott (Byway Books, Hawick)

Scots Magazine, September 1783

'The former ferry site at Brainport', Col. P. Fane OBE, FSA Scot., *The Kist** No. 42

Provisions of the Commissioners of Supply for Argyll

Schedule of Particulars as to Ferries, 1891

Return of Ferries, 1909

Newsletter No. 50, West Highland Steamer Club, October 1994

'The Inveraray Ferry', Donald MacKechnie OBE, MA, *JP, Oban Times* article in the 1980s

Inveraray Castle Archives, with help of Alastair Campbell of Airds and Mrs Rae MacGregor

Inveraray, Jan Lindsay and Mary Cosh

Black's Picturesque Tourist of Scotland (1850s)

Lumsden's Steamboat Companion (1820)

Chapters Thirteen and Fourteen

Provisions of the Commissioners of Supply for Argyll

Morvern Transformed, Philip Gaskell

The Drove Roads of Scotland, A.R.B. Haldane (Nelson, 1952)

Proceedings of the Society of Antiquaries for Scotland

The Third Statistical Account for Scotland

Scottish Studies, Vol. 5 (1961)

Working Boats of Britain, Eric McKee

'The Origin of the "Road to the Isles" ', paper by Jane Dawson, University of Edinburgh

A History of Clan Campbell, vol. 1, Alastair Campbell of Airds

Chapter Fifteen

The Drove Roads of Scotland, A.R.B. Haldane (Nelson, 1952)

The Long Road: A Guide to Jura, Revd Peter Youngson (ed.)

Provisions of the Commissioners of Supply for Argyll

Chapter Sixteen

Correspondence between the Duke of Argyll and his chamberlain on Tiree
in the early 1800s

The Drove Roads of Scotland, A.R.B. Haldane (Nelson, 1952)

Transcripts of Eric Cregeen's conversations on Coll and Tiree

Notes by Capt. and Mrs William Robertson (Mrs Robertson is the
granddaughter of Tearlach Mor)

Report of the Commissioners for Highland Roads, 1805

Chapter Seventeen

'Small Ferries of the West Loch', Hilary Giles, *The Kist** No. 44

'Further Notes on the West Loch Ferries', Duncan Campbell, The Kist*
No. 45

Kilberry Church and Parish, Miss Marion Campbell of Kilberry FSA, FSA
Scot.

A Little Spot in Scotland, Duncan MacDougall

Provisions of the Commissioners of Supply for Argyll

Schedule of Ferries, 1891

---

*The Kist is the biannual publication of the Natural History and Antiquarian Society of Mid-
Argyll.

INDEX